Nature's Beauty in Appliqué

PRETTY AND PRACTICAL PROJECTS

Susan Taylor Propst

Martingale®
& COMPANY

Nature's Beauty in Appliqué: Pretty and Practical Projects
© 2012 by Susan Taylor Propst

Martingale®
& COMPANY

That Patchwork Place®

That Patchwork Place® is an imprint of
Martingale & Company®.

Martingale & Company
19021 120th Ave. NE, Ste. 102
Bothell, WA 98011-9511 USA
www.martingale-pub.com

Printed in China
17 16 15 14 13 12   8 7 6 5 4 3 2 1

**Library of Congress Cataloging-in-Publication Data
is available upon request.**

ISBN: 978-1-60468-079-9

Mission Statement

Dedicated to providing quality products
and service to inspire creativity.

Credits

President & CEO: Tom Wierzbicki

Editor in Chief: Mary V. Green

Design Director: Paula Schlosser

Managing Editor: Karen Costello Soltys

Technical Editor: Ellen Pahl

Copy Editor: Sheila Chapman Ryan

Production Manager: Regina Girard

Cover & Text Designer: Shelly Garrison

Illustrator: Laurel Strand

Photographer: Brent Kane

Special thanks to
Amy Moeller of Snohomish, Washington, and
Howard and Theresa Holman of Snohomish,
Washington, for generously allowing us to
photograph at their beautiful homes.

Acknowledgments

My greatest appreciation goes to all of the editors and staff at Martingale & Company who are so helpful, patient, and wonderful to work with. They take my manuscript and make it so much better!

Many thanks to my husband, who gives me his full support and doesn't complain when I buy fabric but rather encourages me. Thank you also to my daughters, who give me honest feedback and humor me when I need to bounce ideas off of someone.

I truly appreciate all of the encouragement and feedback from friends, students, and readers. I love to see the amazing variety of projects produced from my designs.

And finally, many thanks to my friends who have given helpful advice and tips on the projects, especially Pam Justesen, Roxane Sullivan, Bebe Rasmussen, Debbie Grant, and Chris Marne.

Contents

Introduction

When I wrote my first two books, *Beautiful Blooms* and *Another Season of Beautiful Blooms*, I was living in England and was inspired by the flowers that grow abundantly there. Though I've since relocated back to Colorado, most of the projects in this book were designed while I lived in England, and so that inspiration can still be seen in this book. In those first books, the projects were wall hangings and cushions. Many people enjoy these small-scale projects because they work up fairly quickly, even when hand appliquéd. And the cushions, while decorative, are also useful.

For this book, I decided to continue in that vein; however, I've expanded the range of small and useful items. There are nine projects: one wall hanging, two sizes of tote bags, a table runner, place mats, neck-roll cushion, square cushion, zippered bag, and a rotary-cutter case. As before, the projects don't take a long time to complete, and they make exceptional gifts. Additionally, they can be simplified and made even more quickly when constructed from printed fabric without the appliqué.

All of the projects were inspired by a larger wall hanging that I made featuring a scene with a swan. The inspiration for that quilt came from a photo my husband took at Loch Ness in Scotland. The day we visited the loch, the wind had whipped up a little and the waves could easily have been misidentified as the famous monster. Later, when I had completed the swan wall hanging, I happened to have it turned upside down and noticed that the reflection in the water looked very much like images people have produced of the Loch Ness monster. That's when I decided to call the design "Swan and Nessie."

The patterns for the smaller projects are provided full size, and there's a layout diagram for the larger quilt on page 94. You can re-create a quilt very similar to "Swan and Nessie" using the patterns throughout the book, if desired. The mountains and tree trunks are easy enough to re-create without a specific pattern.

Even though most of the samples are hand appliquéd, these patterns will work equally well for fusible appliqué. If you're new to either type of appliqué, I've included instructions for both methods starting on page 12. Since quilting stitches are a great way to enhance the appliqué, I've also included quilting suggestions for some of the designs. The appliquéd flowers and leaves on the smaller projects also appear in the large wall hanging, so you have the opportunity to see different color options for some of the designs. Have fun making the flowers in colors to match your decor. Don't worry about whether the colors are true to nature as long as they're colors you like. Make these projects your own, and enjoy creating items that you and others can use!

"Swan and Nessie" large wall hanging, 49½" x 39". While there wasn't space
to include the complete quilt instructions in this book, each of the projects
is derived from some part of this larger design. If you like the central image,
there's a smaller wall hanging on page 29 that features the swan oval, or see the
reduced "Swan and Nessie" layout on page 94 if you're feeling adventuresome!

Choosing Fabrics

It's always best to use good quality, 100% cotton fabrics. For appliqué, cotton is easy to use because it doesn't slip around easily and it will finger crease. If the appliqué pieces are small or tricky, I suggest using tightly woven cotton, such as a batik, because it will be less likely to fray. Thicker or heavier-weight fabrics are difficult to use for intricate appliqué pieces. For the backing fabric, use the same quality cotton fabric as you would use for the front of the quilt or cushion.

BACKGROUND FABRICS

The background fabric should support the appliqué but not overwhelm it. There are two things to consider when selecting the background. The first is that it should contrast with the appliqué; this can usually be best achieved by differences in value. If the appliquéd flowers are medium value, use a light or dark value for the background. If the background is pieced or the appliqué extends into the border, then you'll need to be strategic about where to place certain fabrics so they'll be visible. In "Iris Table Runner" shown below, the petals of the iris are pale and wouldn't show up well on a light background. Using a dark fabric behind the flower provides the contrast needed for the flower to stand out. The bud, which is a dark color, has light fabric behind it, which in turn allows it to be visible.

The second consideration when choosing background fabric is the texture of the print. While solid fabrics are a safe choice, a fabric with texture adds dimension to the piece. Just be careful that the fabric is not so busy that the appliqué gets lost. Usually fabrics with too much color or value contrast won't make good background fabrics.

The fabrics on the top are more suitable background choices than the busy fabrics on the bottom.

In "Swan Wall Hanging" shown below, I found two wonderful batiks in dark blue and green with a swirling print and used them for the light and dark portions of the water. They're perfect for adding depth and movement to the background.

Careful choices of background fabric allow flowers to stand out.

Batiks add texture and interest to backgrounds.

I find that it's particularly beneficial to use a design wall to audition fabrics before committing to them. It helps to step back and see how the fabrics work together and weed out any fabrics that obviously don't belong.

It's very tempting sometimes to choose a fabric that's the right motif, such as a print that contains grass, as a background for a flower. However, it's probably more important to choose a *color* that blends and works with the other fabrics in the piece. It can be quite jarring if one portion of the appliqué has a vastly different color that doesn't fit in with the rest. If you can't find a fabric with the image you're looking for in the right color, it's better to select a fabric of the right color. For example, a green batik or tone-on-tone print might work very well for a leaf or shrub. You can always add detail at the quilting stage.

If you don't want an appliqué piece to particularly stand out from the surrounding pieces, try to pick fabrics that share enough color so that the colors blend at the edges. This provides a soft transition between pieces.

The fabrics on the bottom are similar in tone, so the transition between them isn't obvious.

There's a wide selection of landscape fabric available. By that, I mean fabrics that are designed to look like parts of a landscape or that work well to suggest part of a landscape. However, sometimes the color or scale isn't quite right, so I don't always try to find a fabric that is an actual depiction of the portion of the landscape. Rather, I look for a fabric that fits in with the rest of the landscape. Consider both printed fabrics and batiks.

A selection of fabrics suitable for landscapes. Both printed fabrics and batiks work well.

An appliquéd landscape such as "Swan and Nessie" shown on page 7 is often more successful if most of the bright fabrics are in the foreground. As your eye moves towards the back of the scene, the colors tend to get less bright. There's no substitute for trying a fabric out to see if it works, but try to avoid getting so attached to a particular print that you use it even if it really doesn't work with the rest of the fabrics. In other words, keep an open mind and see where your fabric stash can take you, but let the project tell you what's needed.

FABRICS FOR APPLIQUÉ PIECES

My favorite fabrics for appliqué are hand-dyed fabrics—these are the foundation of my appliqué stash. They have a higher thread count and a finer feel than many printed fabrics, which makes the appliqué process easier. The subtle color variations also provide a bit of texture that solid colors don't. There's a wide range of colors available, so you should have no problem finding a fabric to represent most leaves and flowers.

Subtle tone-on-tone fabrics are also good options for appliqués, and sometimes it's fun to use stronger prints, particularly when the print suggests the texture of the flower or leaf to be appliquéd. If you use fabrics that have a strong print, just make sure that they stand out from the other pieces around them.

For "Dahlia Tote Bag" (detail shown below), I found a print that was yellow with orange lines radiating from a center. I fussy cut the appliqué pieces so that the lines radiate from the center of the flower. The result is very effective and I only needed one fabric for all of the petals.

Fussy cutting the petals from one fabric
allows each one to stand out.

A Note about the Color Keys

In the provided color keys, I've listed the fabric colors and values that I used in each project. When I describe a fabric as "pale," I consider that to be lighter than "light."

Effect of Lighting on Color

The use of different types of lighting makes the selection of fabrics challenging. In particular, the recent trend toward the use of compact fluorescent lamps (CFLs) adds to the challenge. The fluorescent bulbs change the appearance of colors, and some colors can change drastically. In addition, some CFLs are closer to daylight than others. I have an inexpensive CFL in my sewing room as well as a daylight lamp. The reasoning behind this is that most of the bulbs in the rest of the house are now CFLs. When I make fabric choices, I want the combinations to look good in all rooms, daylight or nighttime. When I select fabric, I try to work during the day and pick what looks good in natural light, and then close the curtains and turn on the fluorescent light to make sure everything still looks good together. It's amazing how completely different some fabric colors will look, and often some fabric choices have to be changed to make sure that the quilt will look good in any light.

PAINTING FABRIC

If all else fails, painting fabric is a wonderful option. If you have a print that you like but the color isn't quite right, you can use transparent paint to alter the color without losing the detail of the print. For transparent washes, I like to use Setacolor transparent paints. They don't significantly alter the texture of the fabric, and if not applied too heavily, they allow the pattern to show through. I had a wonderful fabric that looked like the ground that I wanted, but it was a bit bright. I used a transparent brown wash to tone down the fabric.

Swatch on the left is toned down with brown transparent paint, applied heaviest in the lower right.

To do a transparent wash you need your fabric, a brush, some plastic to protect your table, water, and transparent paint. Start by testing one or more scraps of the fabric until you get the look you desire.

For a light wash, wet the fabric first and then brush the paint all over the fabric. You can apply the paint uniformly, but even if it doesn't go on perfectly even, that may provide a more interesting look. Keep in mind that the fabric will look much darker when wet than it will when it dries. Don't worry if it's not dark or changed enough on your first application—you can always add more paint, but it's difficult to remove extra paint once it's dried.

You can also paint a portion of a fabric so that the appliqué piece has multiple tones, like I did with the purple dahlias in the lower-left corner of the large wall hanging on page 7. This technique works well if the fabric is wet before the paint is applied. Just note that the paint will flow into the fabric further than you might expect. It's best to practice this technique before you try it on the last scrap of your chosen fabric. It's easier if you paint the fabric before you cut it. Wet an area that's about the size of the petal or other appliqué piece that you want; then brush the contrasting color onto one end and let it flow. Once it dries, you can decide where you want to fussy cut the petal from your painted fabric.

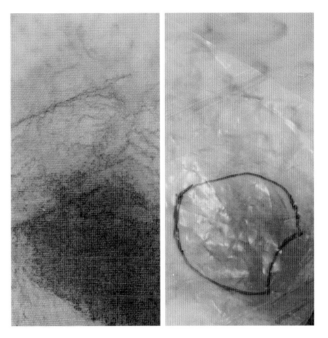

The fabric on the left was wet when the paint was applied, resulting in a slightly different appearance with more spread. The painted fabric on the right has an outline on a plastic overlay showing a possible fussy-cutting position.

Once the fabric is painted to your satisfaction, you'll need to heat set the colors. This is a very important step and usually doesn't involve much more than pressing with a hot iron for a small amount of time. The paint that you choose should come with directions for how to heat set the colors; follow the manufacturer's instructions carefully.

The Appliqué Process

These instructions describe my preferred techniques for hand appliqué, as well as turned-edge appliqué and fusible appliqué. I enjoy hand appliqué, but occasionally I combine methods. The patterns for the projects are adaptable to other methods. If you plan to use a different appliqué technique, keep in mind that the patterns do not include seam allowances and the shapes have *not* been reversed.

CREATING A PLACEMENT GUIDE

The first step is to create a guide for placing the appliqués on the background fabric. Rather than tracing the design directly onto the fabric, I prefer to trace the design onto a plastic or vinyl overlay. It's easier to trace onto plastic, and you don't have to worry about covering or removing any marks on the background fabric.

You can purchase sheets of clear plastic or lightweight vinyl yardage for this purpose, or you can recycle plastic. The plastic needs to be fairly firm and large enough to contain the entire appliqué design. Dry-cleaner bags are a bit too thin, but I have successfully used the plastic wrapping from new shirts. For smaller projects, you can cut open a plastic page protector.

With larger appliqué pieces, such as the large wall hanging shown on page 7, I use a very lightweight interfacing rather than plastic because it's more manageable for larger projects and can be pieced together. It's a bit more difficult to see through though, particularly when adjacent pieces have similar value and color. Use a permanent marker to trace the entire design onto the overlay, including the numbers on each appliqué shape and any border lines, if provided.

One additional significant advantage to using the overlay is that you can turn the overlay over to see the reverse of the pattern. This is helpful when preparing the freezer-paper templates discussed next.

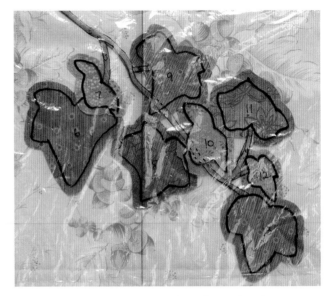

The appliqué pieces have been placed on the background using the overlay as a guide.

PREPARING THE APPLIQUÉS

You'll need to make a freezer-paper template for each appliqué piece. To do this, flip the overlay so that you see the reverse of the pattern. If you're not working on a light surface, you may need to slip a sheet of white paper under the overlay so that you can see the lines better.

1. Lay the freezer paper on top of the reversed pattern, matte side up, and trace around each numbered shape. Write the number of each piece on the shape. Usually you don't need to leave space around the pieces, but if an appliqué piece runs under another piece, you'll have to trace the lower piece separately.

2. Cut out each template on the marked line. Do not add seam allowances.

3. Place each shape, shiny side down, on the wrong side of the chosen appliqué fabric. Using a hot, dry iron, press the freezer-paper templates onto the fabrics. Cut around each piece, leaving a seam allowance of approximately ³⁄₁₆".

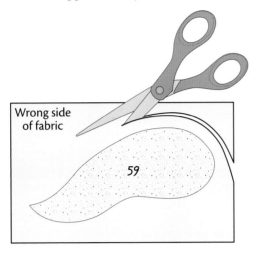

If the freezer paper doesn't adhere well to the fabric, baste around the edges of the freezer paper by hand or machine after ironing the freezer paper to the fabric. Once the piece is appliquéd, the basting is easily removed.

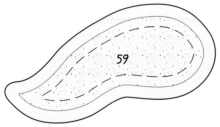

POSITIONING AND STITCHING THE APPLIQUÉS

1. Prepare the background piece as instructed for the individual project. For some of the designs, you may need to piece the background first or add borders because the appliqués extend onto them.

2. Position the overlay on the background piece, right side up. Follow the project instructions for aligning the overlay on the background.

3. Slide appliqué piece 1 under the overlay so that it's aligned beneath the corresponding outline of the design. Remove the overlay. Baste or pin the appliqué in place. If you baste, make sure the

stitching is not within the ¼" seam allowance, which will be turned under. If pinning, use ¾" appliqué pins.

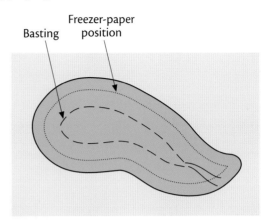

4. With the thread still on the spool, thread a size 10 or 11 straw or milliner's needle with a 50- or 60-weight cotton thread in a color that matches the appliqué. If you can't find an exact color match, choose a thread color that's slightly darker or use a neutral color (gray or beige) that matches the value of the appliqué fabric. Cut the thread, preferably no longer than the distance from your elbow to your fingertips. Thread longer than this tends to tangle and wear thin. Knot the end of the thread that you just cut.

Knotting Your Thread

It's best to use the thread as it comes off the spool because it provides smoother stitching and less tangling. By threading the needle, and then cutting the thread, you don't lose track of which end should be knotted.

5. If possible, begin stitching along the straightest edge of the appliqué. If you're right-handed, you'll probably find it easiest to stitch in a counterclockwise direction, and if you're left-handed, stitch in a clockwise direction. Using the needle, turn under the first ½" or so of seam allowance using the freezer paper as a guide. Don't try to turn under too much at one time, just a little

more than you're going to stitch. It's also important to avoid stabbing at the seam allowance with the tip of the needle, which can cause the fabric to fray. Bring the needle up from the background fabric just under the turned-under edge of the appliqué piece. Insert the needle through the appliqué at the very edge of the appliqué shape.

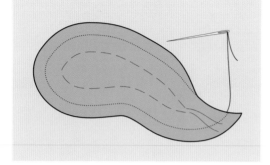

6. Insert the needle back down through the background fabric at or very near where the thread came out, and then back up a little less than ⅛" away, catching the edge of the folded appliqué fabric. You should aim for approximately 12 stitches per inch.

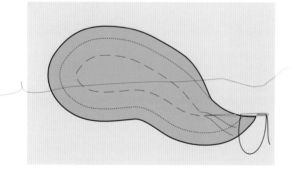

7. Continue stitching all the way around the appliqué piece in this manner. When done properly, the stitches on the back should look almost like a continuous line.

   When an edge or portion of an appliqué piece will be covered by another piece (i.e., a higher-numbered piece), you shouldn't appliqué that portion. You can, however, baste the edge without

turning it under. For example, in the tulip illustration below, the red edges of pieces 4, 5, and 6 are not turned under and appliquéd because they'll be under piece 7. The red edge of piece 7 is turned under and appliquéd.

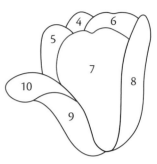

8. When finished, bring the needle to the back, make a small knot close to the fabric, and snip the thread.

9. Remove the freezer paper by carefully slitting the background fabric behind the appliqué piece and slipping it out. Use tweezers to help grab the paper, if needed. You can also remove the freezer paper through an unstitched opening about ½" to 1" before you finish the appliqué stitching.

10. Position and stitch the remaining appliqués to the background in numerical order.

STITCHING POINTS AND CURVES

Points and curves can pose an appliqué challenge. Here are some helpful hints for stitching these tricky areas.

Outside Points

1. For crisp points, trim the seam allowances a bit closer to the stitching line, but leave enough fabric to turn under. A scant ⅛" is usually about right.

2. Turn under only the side of the point you're stitching. Don't worry about the other side yet. As you approach the point, take slightly smaller stitches. You'll be folding the seam allowance into a smaller area, and smaller stitches will keep the seam allowance contained, preventing it from poking out between the stitches.

3. At the point, take one stitch, and then take another in the same place. This will help hold the seam down on the first side of the point while you push under the seam allowance for the second side.

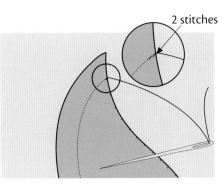

4. If there is still too much fabric at the point to turn under, trim a small amount away, but be careful not to trim too close. With the edge of the needle, sweep the seam allowances for the second side of the point under. Use the thumb on your non-sewing hand to help crease the edge and keep the fabric under. You may need to tug gently on the thread as you do this to help retain the point.

5. Stitch with smaller stitches until you're past the bulkiest part, and then resume stitching as normal.

Inside Points

1. Stitch until you're close to the inside point, and then clip straight into the point, all the way up to the stitching line.

2. Gently use the length of the needle to turn under the seam allowances on the side on which you're stitching. Try to disturb the point as little as possible to keep the fabric from fraying.

3. Carefully appliqué up to the point. This is where a very fine needle comes in handy, because it's less likely to split the fabric and cause fraying.

4. Take an additional stitch at the point, taking a slightly deeper bite into the appliqué fabric if necessary (no more than one thread's width).

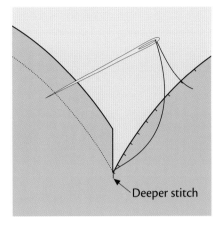

5. Gently turn under the fabric on the other side of the point and continue appliquéing.

Concave Curves

Very gentle concave curves may be easier to turn under if you simply trim the seam allowances a bit closer. However, if you find that you can't turn under the curve smoothly, make small clips along the curve. It's better to make several short clips than fewer long clips. On deep curves, however, you can clip all the way to the stitching line if necessary. When the curve has been clipped, use the length of the needle and sweep the seam allowances under. Avoid stabbing at the seam allowances because this will cause the fabric to fray.

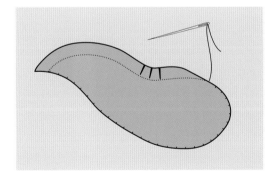

something to adhere to. When it's time to remove the freezer paper, you can mist the seam allowance with a small amount of water to soften the glue.

Starch. Spray some spray starch into a small container. Using a brush, paint starch on all of the fabric that extends past the freezer-paper template (the seam allowances). Fold the seam allowances over and use a hot iron to press them in place. If you choose, you can remove the freezer paper before stitching.

TURNED-EDGE APPLIQUÉ

With turned-edge appliqué, the raw edges are turned under before you position and stitch the pieces. This involves a bit more preparation, but I use it for large appliqué pieces. It's much easier to align the appliqués and it makes the stitching go a bit faster. When the pieces are small or intricate, I prefer to use freezer-paper templates and needle-turn the edges under as I stitch, as previously discussed.

1. Prepare the freezer-paper templates as you would for needle-turn appliqué, ironing them onto the wrong side of the fabric. Trim the seam allowances to about 3/16".

2. Fold the seam allowances to the wrong side using the freezer paper as a guide. You only want to turn the edges that need to be appliquéd; do not turn edges that will lie underneath another appliqué piece. Use one of the following methods to hold the turned seam allowances.

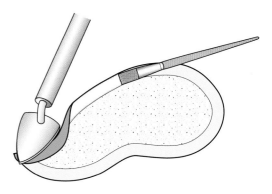

Basting. Fold the seam allowances over and run a basting stitch in the seam allowance, stitching through the two layers of fabric and the freezer paper, to hold the turned-back seam allowance in place.

Glue. Using a glue stick, apply glue to the freezer paper along the seam allowance area, keeping within about 1/4" from the cut edges. At corners or points, you may need to apply glue to the first fabric that is folded back so that the fabric folded back on the other side of the corner or point has

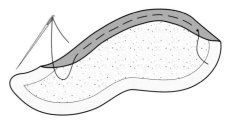

Once the appliqué pieces are ready, placement will be easy because the turned edges should line up exactly with the lines on the overlay.

FUSIBLE APPLIQUÉ

Usually I try to design appliqué so that it can be done fairly easily by hand, and all of the instructions refer to using freezer-paper templates. However, sometimes it's quicker and easier to use fusible appliqué. I used fusible appliqué for the water reflection on the large wall hanging, and you can use this method for any of the projects in the book.

For fusible appliqué, you need to purchase a fusible web. There are a number of brands available. Just be sure to choose a lightweight fusible for these projects. You can combine fusible appliqué with freezer-paper appliqué by following these directions for those pieces you want to fuse. I suggest prewashing your fabrics for this method since fusible webs usually adhere better to prewashed fabrics.

1. Follow the steps in "Creating a Placement Guide" on page 12 to make an overlay if you've not already done so.

2. Turn the overlay to the wrong side so that you see the reverse of the pattern. If you're not working on a light surface, it will be helpful to put a sheet of white paper under the overlay so that you can see the lines, or use a light box.

3. Place the fusible over the pattern with the paper side up. If your fusible has two paper sides, make sure that the side with the fusible attached is on top. Trace around each appliqué piece, leaving ¼" to ½" around each piece.

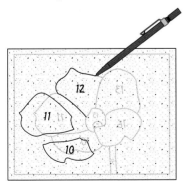

4. Loosely cut around the traced pieces, leaving a little extra around the drawn lines.

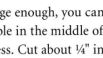

5. If the piece is large enough, you can remove some of the fusible in the middle of the piece to minimize stiffness. Cut about ¼" inside the drawn line.

6. Following the manufacturer's instructions, fuse the web pieces to the wrong side of the chosen appliqué fabrics.

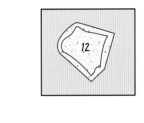

Protect Your Ironing Surface

I like to put a piece of paper on my ironing surface to protect it from any extra bits of fusible web that may have strayed onto my ironing board. You can use regular paper or parchment paper. If you plan to do a lot of fusible appliqué, a nonstick appliqué pressing sheet would be an even better idea.

7. Cut carefully along the traced lines on the paper backing. Make sure that the fusible is adhered to the fabric. If not, carefully press again with your iron. Then peel the paper from the fusible appliqué.

8. Position the appliqué piece where you want it on the background and fuse in place. If you're using an overlay for placement, make sure you remove the overlay before you fuse the appliqué in place. Continue fusing until you have all of the fusible appliqués in place.

9. The raw edges of the appliqué pieces will need to be finished. I prefer a zigzag stitch rather than a satin stitch since it's less noticeable. Outline all of the edges with a zigzag stitch in thread that's a similar color to the fabric, backstitching a few stitches at the beginning and end. You can quilt or embroider on top of the fused pieces as with any other appliqué pieces.

CONSTRUCTING APPLIQUÉ UNITS

For many of the projects in this book, you can construct parts of the design as a unit before appliquéing them to the background. This often makes placement or piecing easier. When the instructions indicate unit construction, you'll appliqué the specified pieces to each other first, and then appliqué the entire unit to the background. Some pieces need to be appliquéd to each other before they're stitched to other pieces; these are marked on the patterns with an arrow. The iris pattern is an example. When the pieces are stitched together before either piece is stitched to the background, the two pieces form an edge that's easier to turn under.

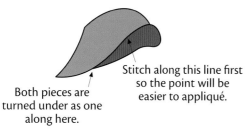

Both pieces are turned under as one along here.

Stitch along this line first so the point will be easier to appliqué.

When constructing units with more than two pieces, it can be difficult to get the pieces to fit together correctly. Draw the pattern for the entire unit on white tissue paper, and then trim the tissue paper so that it's only slightly larger than the edges of the unit. Then use the tissue paper as a guide for placement of the pieces in the unit. I like to baste the pieces to the tissue paper because it helps them stay in the correct position. Stitch the pieces where they meet, stitching through the tissue paper as if you were stitching to the background fabric. Don't stitch the outside edges.

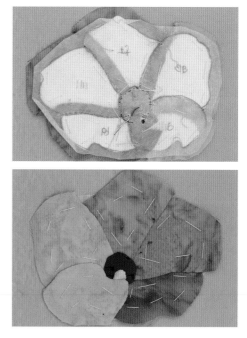

Individual petals have been stitched to tissue paper and the unit is ready to be stitched to the background.

When all the pieces for the unit have been stitched together, remove the tissue paper. Don't remove the freezer paper yet; you still need that as a guide for stitching the edges. Stitch the outer edges of the unit to the background fabric. Then remove any basting and slit the background fabric behind the unit to remove the freezer paper.

MAKING BIAS STRIPS AND STEMS

You can treat stems like any other appliqué piece, creating a freezer-paper template for them. However, for a consistent-width stem, make a bias strip instead.

1. On a single layer of the stem fabric, align the 45° line of your rotary-cutting ruler with the selvage edge so that the ruler's straight edge extends completely across the fabric. Cut along the edge of the ruler with your rotary cutter.

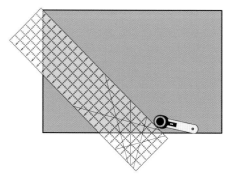

2. To determine the width of bias strip needed, multiply the desired finished width of the strip by 2, and then add ¾". For example, if the finished strip needs to be ¼" wide, the strip should be cut 1¼" wide (2 x ¼" = ½"; ½" + ¾" = 1¼"). Measuring from the cut edge, cut strips the determined width, cutting as many strips as you need to achieve the desired length.

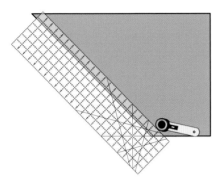

3. Press each strip in half lengthwise, wrong sides together. Stitch ¼" from the raw edges.

4. Fold under the seam allowances at the stitching line, making sure that the stitching does not show. Press firmly.

5. If the finished strip is narrower than ¼", trim the seam allowances so that the cut edges do not show on the front. Because the edges are on the bias, the fabric will not fray.

6. Position the strip in place and appliqué along both edges. The seam-allowance side will not curve as easily as the other side, so place this side on the inside of any curves.

Quilting and Sewing Basics

Review this section for information on adding borders, quilting, and finishing your quilts. I've also included instructions for other sewing techniques that you'll need to complete the cushions and tote bags, such as installing a zipper, adding piping, and making bag handles.

ADDING BORDERS

The width and length of all border strips are specified in the project cutting instructions, but I strongly recommend that you measure your quilt top as described in this section before cutting the borders. My measurements are based on cutting pieces precisely and taking an exact ¼" seam allowance, but try as we might to achieve perfection, variances do occur.

1. Measure the width of the quilt project near the top edge, through the horizontal center, and near the bottom edge. If these three measurements are within ¼" of each other, make a note of the center

measurement and continue with step 2. If not, check your seam allowances to make sure they're accurate and restitch any that aren't.

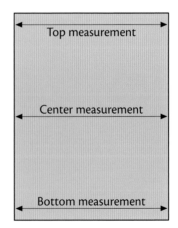

2. From the border fabric, cut two strips the length of the center measurement. I often just square up one end of my border strips, lay the strips across the center of the project with the squared-up

ends aligned with the project left edge, and cut the opposite ends even with the right edge of the project.

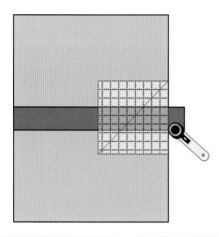

3. Stitch one strip to the top edge of the project top and the other to the bottom, easing to fit as necessary. Press the seam allowances toward the border strips.

4. Repeat step 1 to measure the length of the project top near the left and right edges and through the vertical center, including the top and bottom borders. Square up the piece if necessary. Cut two border strips the length of the center measurement. Or, lay two border strips along the lengthwise center of the project top and trim them as described in step 2. Sew the strips to the sides of the piece. Press the seam allowances toward the border strips.

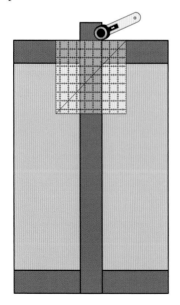

PREPARING THE QUILT SANDWICH

Before you can quilt your project, you must layer the appliquéd top with batting and backing. These layers are often called the quilt "sandwich." For the backing, use a quilting fabric that coordinates with the front and will not show through any light areas.

1. Cut the backing fabric so that it's about 1" larger than the project top on each side. Cut the batting so that it's about ½" larger than the top on each side. Iron the backing fabric and project top to remove any wrinkles.

2. Lay the backing fabric on a smooth surface, wrong side up. Using masking tape, tape at intervals around the edges so that it lies flat. It should be taut but not stretched.

3. Center the batting on top of the backing, and carefully smooth out all wrinkles.

4. Lay the project top on the batting, right side up. Use a ruler to make sure that the corners are square. Then use long basting stitches around the edges, checking as you go to make sure that the top is square.

5. Use small, rustproof safety pins or long basting stitches to baste the remainder of the sandwich together, working in straight lines parallel to the borders to keep your work square.

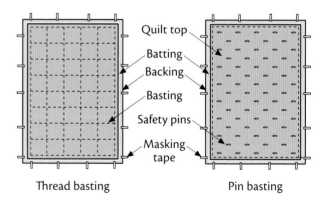

Thread basting   Pin basting

6. Remove the tape. Your sandwich is ready to quilt.

QUILTING

One of the things that I like most about hand appliqué is the dimensional effect created by the seam allowances padding the edges of the pieces. This effect can be further enhanced with quilting. At a minimum, I usually outline quilt around the appliqué pieces. Use a thread color that matches either the background fabric or the appliqué pieces or, if you'll be machine quilting over areas with many fabric colors and don't want the thread to be too obvious, clear monofilament is a good choice.

Quilting can also be used to add detail, such as leaf veins and stamens. When adding detail quilting, you may find it helpful to plan the quilting lines in advance. Make a scale drawing of your project and use colored pencil to mark the quilting lines. Modifications are easy to make at this stage because no stitching has been done. When you're happy with the quilting plan, mark the quilting lines on the fabric and quilt away. Cotton, rayon, and other decorative threads are good for enhancing detail quilting.

Quilting veins in the hosta leaves adds a touch of realism.

If you prefer, as I do, not to mark directly onto the fabric, you can trace your quilting pattern onto a tear-away stabilizer. After drawing the pattern onto the tear-away material, position it on the quilt top, and then quilt on the drawn lines. After the quilting is complete, the tear-away product is easily removed. When you're finished quilting, snip all thread ends, or thread a needle with the ends and hide them in the quilt sandwich. Trim the excess batting and backing even with the edges of the top.

The background areas behind the appliqué pieces are often large enough that they benefit from some quilting. I like to quilt the backgrounds in a way that complements the appliqué rather than using a random allover design.

Parallel lines. Parallel lines are a nice way to quilt a useful item. It doesn't take a lot of time but provides a nice, consistent background that complements the shapes of the appliqué pieces. This type of quilting looks best when it's stitched only on the background area and doesn't continue over the appliqué pieces.

Detail of quilting on "Iris Table Runner." Notice how the lines echo the shapes in the patchwork background.

To create evenly spaced parallel lines, I find that I get the best results by marking the lines with masking tape. If the tape is the same width as the interval between lines, you can mark two lines at a time with each piece of tape. You won't have to mark any lines on the fabric, you can adjust the tape if necessary before starting to quilt, and you can wait until after the layers have been basted to position the tape. However, to avoid sticky residue on your fabric, make sure that you don't apply the tape until you're ready to quilt, and don't leave it on the fabric for more than a day or two.

Free-motion quilting. Any meandering free-motion quilting, such as stippling, can be used to fill in the background. The advantage of a meandering technique is that you don't have to start and stop often, if at all. It also provides a nice background to allow the appliqué to stand out in areas such as clouds and bushes.

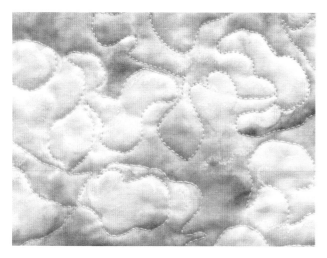

Free-motion stitching lets you mimic the shapes of clouds or other random-shaped background elements.

Side-to-side stippling in the water helps to define the ripples. Stitching across the two colors of water fabric unified the water pieces.

Embellishment quilting. With appliqué quilts, there's always an opportunity to quilt in a way that embellishes the design as well as holding the layers together. In some areas, random stippling will work well, but there are other areas where the appliqué element may suggest other types of quilting.

Quilting stitches add the look of feathers on the swan. The quilting pattern does not have to be extremely detailed and can even be a bit stylized. The suggestion of feathers adds depth to the image of the swan.

The mountains are quilted in a way that defines the contours of the slopes. I prefer to have the quilting recede back into the landscape, so I didn't use fine detail in the mountain quilting.

I used just one piece of fabric for each ivy leaf. By quilting the vein lines, the leaves look more realistic.

MAKING A HANGING SLEEVE

A hanging sleeve will help you display your project on a wall. It can be made from muslin, the backing fabric, or any other fabrics you used in your quilt top.

1. Determine the desired finished width of the sleeve. For the projects in this book, a 3"-wide sleeve should be more than adequate.

2. Cut a strip of fabric twice the finished width of the sleeve plus ½". For a 3" sleeve, that would be 6½". Cut the length 1" shorter than the finished width of the wall hanging.

3. Hem the short ends by folding under approximately ⅜" twice. Stitch ⅛" from the first fold.

4. Press the strip in half lengthwise, wrong sides together and raw edges aligned.

5. Center the sleeve on the back of the wall hanging, aligning the raw edges with the top edge of the wall hanging. Baste in place ¼" from the raw edges through all layers.

6. Add the binding as instructed below. The sleeve raw edge will be enclosed in the binding.

7. Hand blindstitch the bottom of the sleeve to the backing of the wall hanging, making sure the stitches don't go through to the front.

BINDING

The fabric you use for the binding can be the same fabric as the border, or it can be a different fabric that complements the piece. Try to avoid bright colors, though, because they'll draw the eye away from the quilt center.

1. Cut straight-grain or bias binding strips as instructed for the project. Join the strips as shown to make one long piece. Press the seam allowances open.

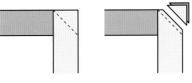

Joining straight-cut strips

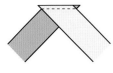

Joining bias-cut strips

2. Press the binding strip in half lengthwise, wrong sides together.

3. With raw edges aligned, place the binding strip at about the center of the bottom edge. "Walk" the binding around the quilt to see whether any of the joining seams will end up at a corner. If they do, move the starting point of the binding so that this no longer occurs. With your walking foot, begin stitching the binding to the quilt, leaving about 4" at the end of the binding unstitched. Use a ¼" seam allowance. When you're ¼" from the first corner, angle the stitching into the corner. Clip the threads and remove the quilt from under the presser foot.

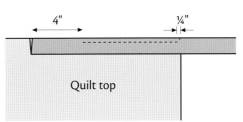

4. Fold the binding up so that the fold makes a 45° angle, and then fold the binding back down onto itself so that the raw edge is aligned with the quilt raw edge. Starting at the folded edge, stitch the binding to the next side of the quilt. Repeat for each corner.

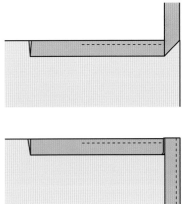

5. Stop sewing about 8" from the starting point. Open up the ends and fold them back at a 45° angle until the folds meet. Mark or finger-press the folds. Open up the folds and, with right sides together, align the diagonal lines. Lift the binding away from the quilt and stitch on the line. Make sure that the

binding fits the unstitched space, and then trim the seam allowances to ¼" and press open. Refold the binding and stitch it in place.

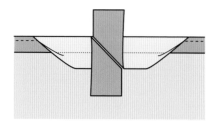

6. Fold the binding to the back of the quilt and hand blindstitch it in place, mitering the corners.

INSTALLING A ZIPPER

The zipper packaging will usually contain instructions, but I've included some basic information you can use.

1. With right sides together, use a ⅝" seam allowance to baste the pieces together where the zipper will go. Press the seam allowances open.

2. Place the zipper face down on the seam, with the coil centered on the seam line. Using a very long basting stitch, baste both long sides of the zipper to the fabric, following the stitching guideline on the zipper tape. I prefer to do this step by hand, but it can be done by machine.

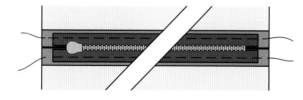

3. Unzip the zipper part of the way to begin stitching so that you don't have to stitch next to the slider. You may have to remove some of the basting stitches from step 2 to move the slider. Stitching from the right side of the fabric and using a zipper foot, topstitch one side of the zipper, maintaining an even distance from the seam. As you get close to the slider, stop with the needle down and raise the presser foot. Move the slider back up to close the zipper. Continue topstitching until you're just past the bottom of the zipper.

Stitching Aid

To keep your topstitching nice and straight and the same distance from the opening on both sides of the zipper, use masking tape as a guide. On the right side, place a strip of ¼"-wide masking tape on both sides of the zipper to mark where the topstitching should be. Then stitch along the outer edge of each piece of the masking tape and remove the tape when you're done.

4. Turn the piece 90° and topstitch across the bottom of the zipper. Turn the piece 90° again and topstitch the remaining side, moving the slider out of the way as necessary.

5. Remove the basting stitches from the zipper and the seam allowance.

Reinforcement

When a zipper will get a lot of use, you can reinforce it by adding a fabric tab to one or both ends. Follow these steps before basting the zipper in place.

1. Cut an additional piece of the backing fabric, 1½" x 4". Fold in half, wrong sides together, so that it measures 1½" x 2".

2. Position the piece so that it's centered over the basted zipper seam, with the raw edges even with the edge of the joined fabric and the folded side toward the center. Baste in place slightly less than ¼" from the edge. When positioning the zipper, place the edge of the zipper pull against the folded edge of the fabric tab rather than all the way to the edge.

3. Repeat with the other side of the zipper if desired. Then continue with the zipper installation.

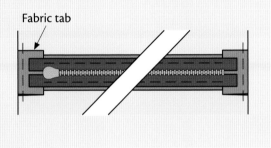

Fabric tab

ADDING PIPING

Piping adds a nice finish to cushions. It's made by wrapping fabric around a length of cording. I usually use ¼"-diameter cotton cording, but you may use a slightly thicker cording if you wish. Just check to be sure that the fabric strip will wrap around the cording and leave at least a ¼" seam allowance. Preshrink cotton cording before making your piping. If you have a piping foot for your machine, this makes applying the piping easier, but a zipper foot will also work.

1. Cut 1¼"-wide strips of fabric for covering the cording. For a square cushion, you can cut straight-grain strips, but if the cushion is round, you'll need to cut bias strips (see page 18).

2. Join the strips in the same manner as for binding (see page 23) to make a length sufficient to go around the cushion plus about 3" extra. Press the seam allowances open.

3. Fold the strip around the cording, aligning the raw edges and with the right side of the fabric on the outside. Pin it in place. Baste close to the cording along the length of the strip. If you're using a piping foot, slide the cording under the groove of the foot with the raw edges of the fabric to the right. If you're using a zipper foot, the needle should be to the left of the foot so that you can stitch as close to the cotton cording as possible.

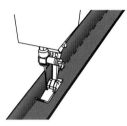

4. Trim the seam allowances ¼" from the basting stitches. Rather than trying to balance the ruler on the piping, it's easier to determine the amount to trim off, and then lay the ruler over the raw edges and cut.

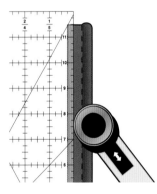

5. Leaving about 1" loose at the beginning, pin the piping along the edges of the right side of the cushion top, aligning the raw edges.

For a square cushion: Begin at the center of the bottom edge and pin the piping in place until you're close to the first corner. Clip the seam allowances when you're ¼" from the corner. This allows you to turn the corner. Turn the piping at the corner as shown and continue pinning. Repeat at each corner.

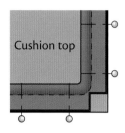

For a round cushion: Begin at the bottom and pin around the top. If necessary, clip the piping seam allowances as you go to allow the piping to lie flat around the curve.

6. When you reach the starting point, trim the piping 1" beyond the beginning. Rip out 1" of the basting stitches at the end of the piping and fold back the unstitched fabric. Cut the end of the exposed cording so that it meets the beginning of the cording. Unfold the turned-back fabric and turn it under about ½" to create a finished edge. Wrap the folded edge around the starting end of the piping.

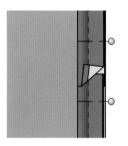

7. Using a piping or zipper foot, baste around the edge of the cushion, following the previous line of stitching.

MAKING BOXED CORNERS

When making cushions and tote bags, there are times when you want to add dimension to a corner. Making a boxed corner gives depth to an otherwise flat item.

Boxed corners create a flat bottom
on tote bags and other items.

1. Fold the corner so that it comes to a point, centering the side seam so that it runs through the point. Press the seam allowances to one side.

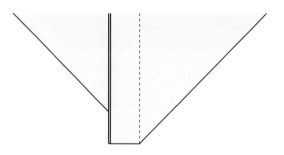

2. The depth of the corner is determined by the length of the seam that's stitched perpendicular to the side seam and its distance from the point. The length of the perpendicular seam is two times the distance from the point. So for example, if you want a depth of 4", the seam needs to be 4" long and 2" from the point. For a tote bag, this would create a bag bottom that's 4" wide. Position a ruler with the edge 2" from the point; there should be 2" on either side of the seam if it's centered correctly.

Align a perpendicular line of the ruler with the stitching of the seam. Mark along the edge of the ruler.

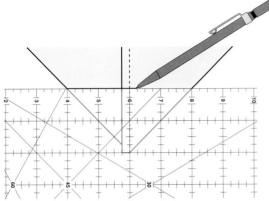

3. Pin the corners together and stitch along the marked line, backstitching at both ends. Repeat the process for each corner that needs to be stitched.

4"

2"

No Need to Trim

I don't trim the points of the triangles off at the corners. The extra fabric adds some rigidity to the corners and I don't have to worry about raw edges after trimming.

MAKING BAG HANDLES

1. Fold each handle strip in half lengthwise with wrong sides together and press. Then open and fold each long edge to the fold (a quarter fold) and press again.

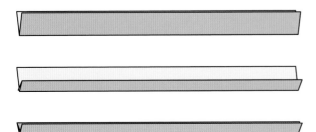

2. Cut a piece of heavy interfacing or batting the same length and width as the finished handle as reinforcement.

3. Open one side of each folded handle strip and place the reinforcement strip between the center fold and one of the quarter folds. Fold the strip back together with the reinforcement strip inside. Topstitch ⅛" from the long folded edges. Use a zigzag or overlock stitch at both ends of the handle.

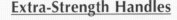

Extra-Strength Handles

To add strength to the handles, use belt webbing in addition to, or instead of, interfacing or batting.

ATTACHING A LABEL

A label is a nice addition to your project, particularly if you've made it as a gift. At a minimum, the label should contain the maker's name, location, date of completion, and washing instructions. Most labels are appliquéd to the back of the project after it's completed (or inside the project if it's a bag or cushion). You can piece it into the backing or lining before the project is done, making it a more permanent part of the project.

Labels add a personal and finishing touch to your project. They can be as simple or elaborate as you like.

SWAN Wall Hanging

Swans are such elegant creatures. After making the larger "Swan and Nessie" quilt, I wanted the focus to be on a single swan in this smaller wall hanging. I found two wonderful ripple batiks to use for the water. If you don't have fabric with ripples, you can use a dark and light hand-dyed fabric, as I did with the large wall hanging on page 7. Don't be afraid to use a dark taupe fabric for the swan. There needs to be a lot of contrast for the shadowed areas.

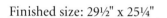

Finished size: 29½" x 25¼"

MATERIALS

All yardages are based on 42"-wide fabric.

⅝ yard of pale-green print for background

½ yard of brown print for outer border

1 fat quarter of light-aqua batik for water

1 fat quarter of dark-green batik for water

¼ yard of green batik for inner border

1 fat eighth of white fabric for swan

Scraps of 4 taupe fabrics for swan

Scraps of 4 green fabrics for leaves

Scraps of 2 turquoise fabrics for bows

Scrap of black fabric for swan

⅓ yard of dark print for binding

1 yard of fabric for backing

31" x 27" piece of batting

Plastic or vinyl for overlay

Freezer paper

CUTTING

All measurements include ¼"-wide seam allowances.

From the pale-green print, cut:
1 rectangle, 18" x 22"

From the green batik, cut:
2 strips, 1½" x 21½"
2 strips, 1½" x 19¼"

From the brown print, cut:
2 strips, 3½" x 23½"
2 strips, 3½" x 25¼"

From the dark print for binding, cut:
3 strips, 2¼" x 42"

APPLIQUÉING THE QUILT CENTER

Refer to "The Appliqué Process" on page 12.

1. Use the pattern on pages 31–34 to make a complete pattern of the swan oval appliqué. Use appliqué pieces 1–25. Trace the complete pattern onto plastic or vinyl to make the overlay.

2. Use the pattern to make freezer-paper templates for the appliqués. Refer to the color key on page 30 to prepare the appliqués from the fabrics indicated.

3. Appliqué pieces 1–25 to the pale-green background rectangle, stitching in numerical order.

4. Remove all freezer-paper templates.

5. Trim the appliquéd rectangle so that it measures 17¼" x 21½".

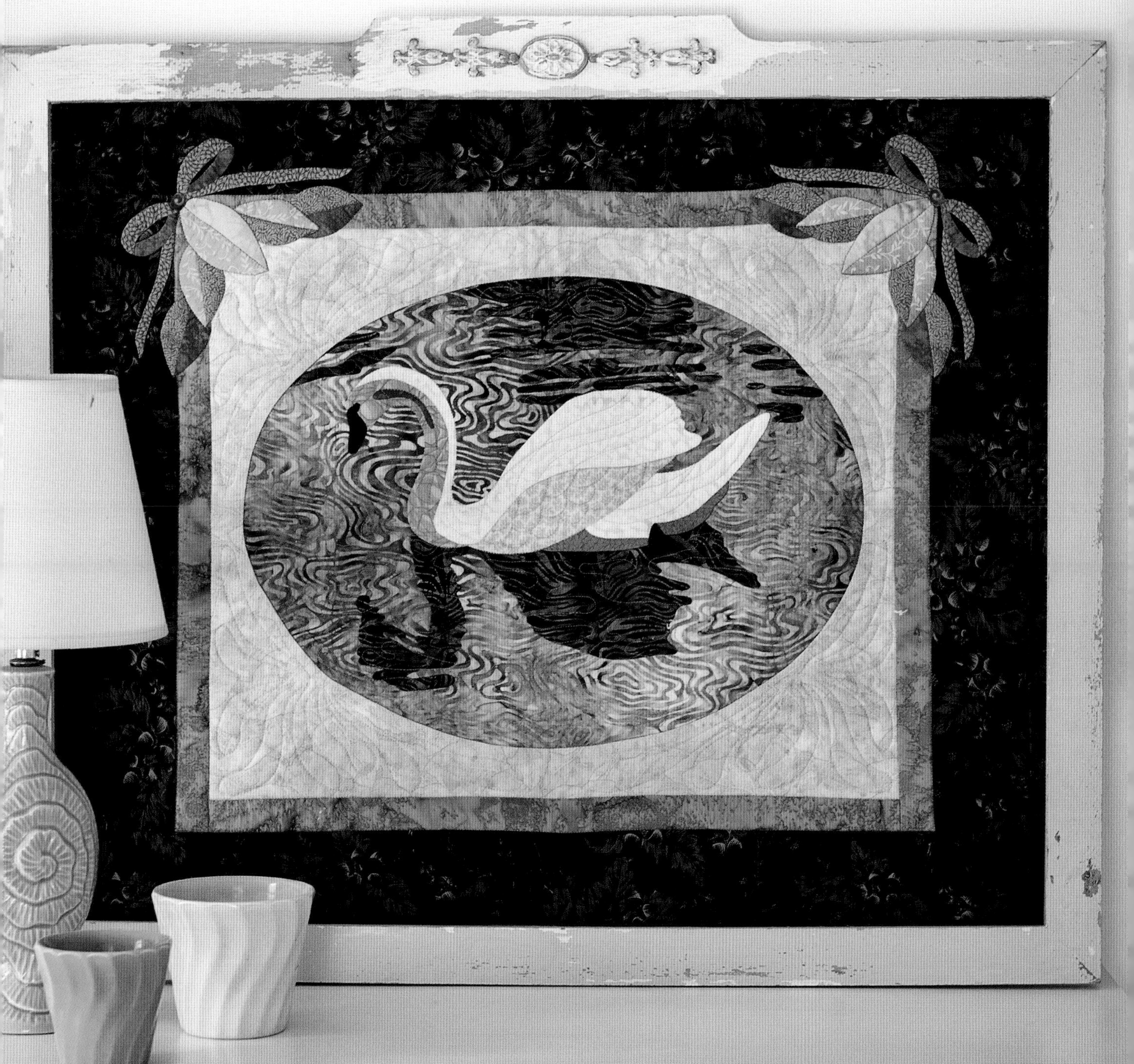

6. Sew the green batik 1½" x 21½" strips to the top and bottom of the appliquéd background. Press the seam allowances toward the borders. Add the green 1½" x 19¼" strips to the sides and press.

7. Sew the brown print 3½" x 23½" strips to the top and bottom of the quilt; press the seam allowances toward the brown borders. Sew the brown 3½" x 25¼" strips to the sides and press.

APPLIQUÉING THE CORNERS

1. Use the pattern on page 35 to make a complete pattern of the leaf cluster and bow for the corner appliqué. Trace the pattern onto plastic or vinyl to make an overlay of the corner appliqué. The pattern is drawn for the right corner. Reverse the pattern and overlay for the left corner.

2. Use the pattern to make freezer-paper templates for the appliqués. Mark an "R" on the freezer-paper templates to indicate that these pieces are to be stitched to the right corner. Refer to the color key at right to prepare the appliqués from the fabrics indicated.

3. Reverse the pattern and make a second set of freezer-paper templates for the appliqués. Mark an "L" on the freezer-paper templates to indicate that these pieces are to be stitched to the left corner. Prepare a second set of appliqués from the fabrics indicated.

4. Beginning with the right corner, appliqué the following pieces together to make units: 1 and 2, 3 and 4, 5 and 6, 7 and 8, 9 and 10, 13 and 14, and 15 and 16. Then repeat this with the left-corner pieces.

5. Appliqué right-corner pieces 1–17 to the upper-right corner, using the right side of the overlay and the border seam lines as a guide for placement. Stitch in numerical order.

6. Repeat step 5 to appliqué left-corner pieces 1–17 to the upper-left corner, using the reversed overlay.

7. Remove all freezer-paper templates.

FINISHING

1. Layer the appliquéd top with batting and backing; baste the layers together.

2. Quilt as desired.

3. Refer to "Binding" on page 23 to finish your quilted piece.

SWAN OVAL COLOR KEY	
Fabric color	**Piece(s)**
Light-aqua batik	1
Dark-green batik	2–16
White	19, 23
Pale taupe	20
Medium taupe	22
Medium-dark taupe	21
Dark taupe	17, 18
Black	24, 25

CORNER COLOR KEY	
Fabric color	**Piece(s)**
Pale green	9
Light green	3, 7, 10
Medium green	1, 4, 5, 8
Medium-dark green	2, 6
Turquoise	11, 12, 14, 16
Medium-dark turquoise	13, 15, 17

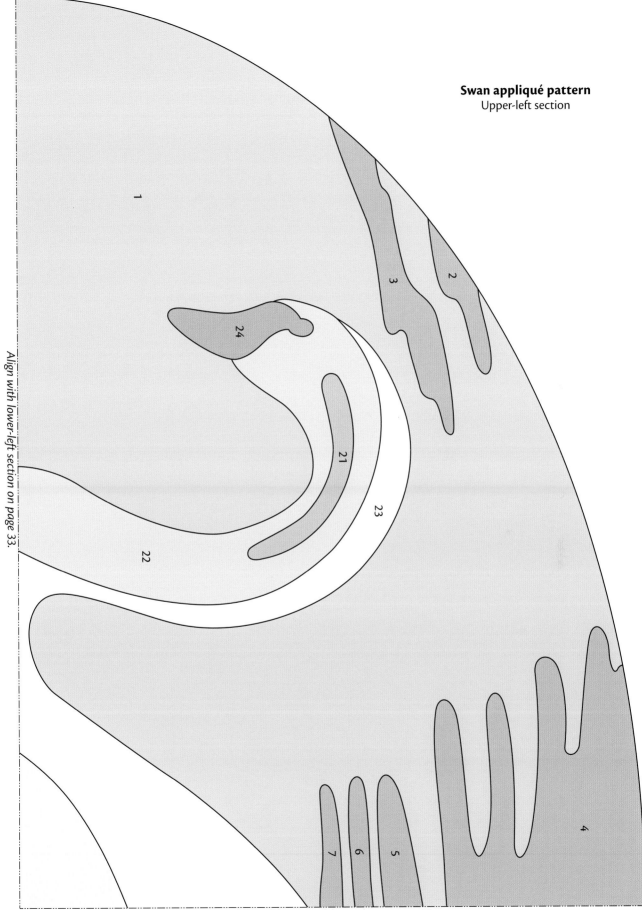

Align with lower-left section on page 33.

Swan appliqué pattern
Upper-left section

Align with upper-right section on page 32.

SWAN WALL HANGING

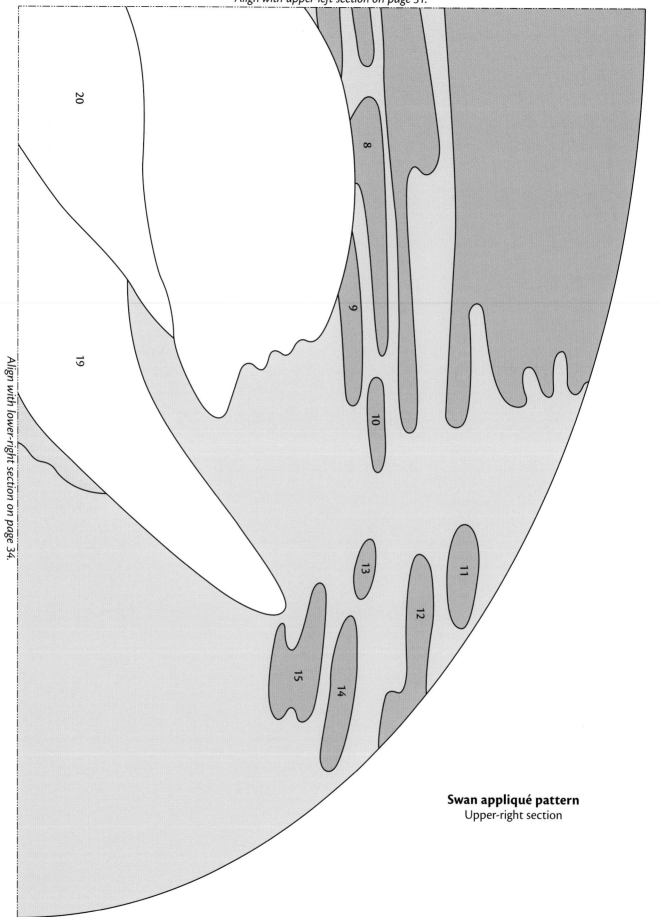

Align with upper-left section on page 31.

Align with lower-right section on page 34.

20

19

8

9

10

13

11

12

15

14

Swan appliqué pattern
Upper-right section

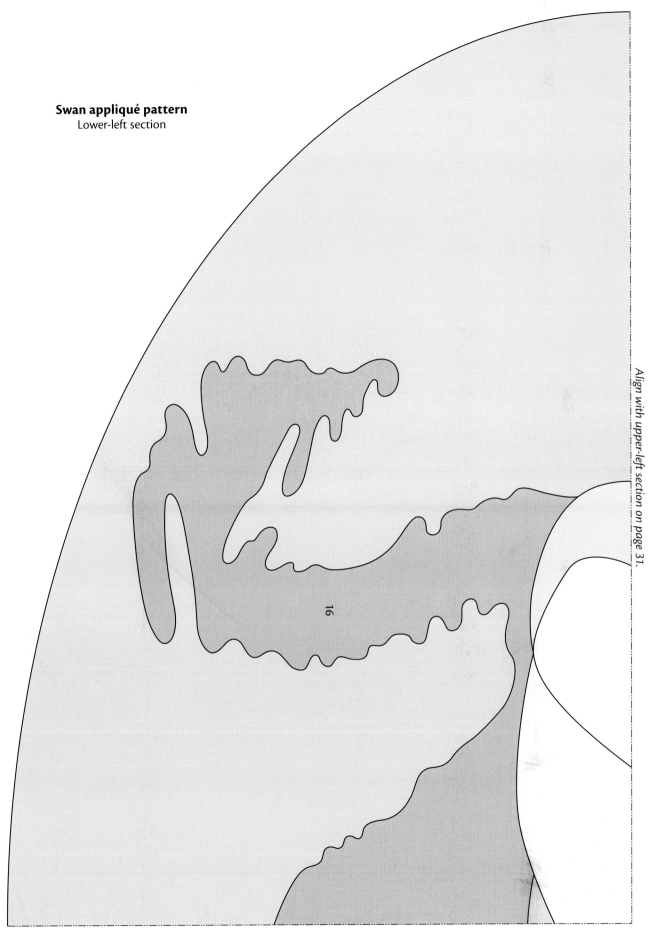

Swan appliqué pattern
Lower-left section

16

Align with upper-left section on page 31.

Align with lower-right section on page 34.

Align with lower-left section on page 33.

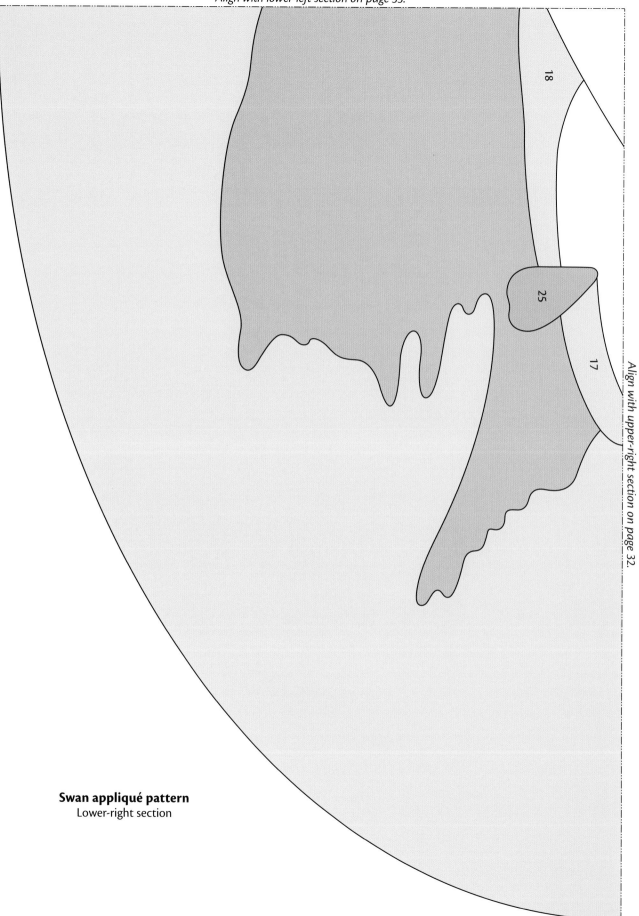

18

25

17

Align with upper-right section on page 32.

Swan appliqué pattern
Lower-right section

SWAN WALL HANGING

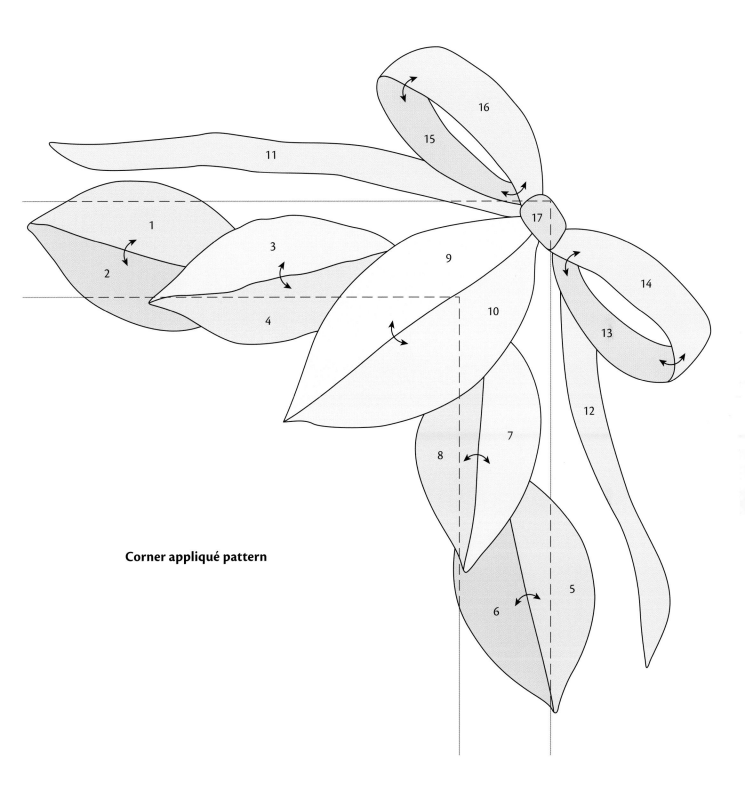

Corner appliqué pattern

IRIS Table Runner

I think that irises are stunning flowers. I couldn't resist making a table runner featuring irises that I could display on my table year-round. The nice thing about combining a pieced background with appliqué is that you can use different colors in the background to help the appliqué pieces stand out. For irises with light petals, a dark background allows the flowers to sparkle.

Finished size: 16" x 40"

MATERIALS

All yardages are based on 42"-wide fabric.

⅝ yard of purple fabric for inner border and binding

⅜ yard of floral print for outer border

1 fat quarter of dark-purple fabric for background

1 fat quarter of ivory fabric for background

Scraps of at least 4 different green fabrics for leaves, stems, and buds

Scraps of at least 3 different pale-mauve fabrics for irises

Scraps of at least 3 medium- to dark-mauve fabrics for irises and buds

Scrap of gold fabric for flower centers

⅝ yard of fabric for backing

17" x 41" piece of batting

Plastic or vinyl for overlay

Freezer paper

CUTTING

All measurements include ¼"-wide seam allowances.

From the dark-purple fabric, cut:
2 squares, 9¼" x 9¼"

From the ivory fabric, cut:
2 squares, 9¼" x 9¼"

From the floral print, cut:
2 strips, 3¼" x 32½"
2 strips, 3¼" x 8½"
4 squares, 3¼" x 3¼"
4 squares, 1½" x 1½"

From the purple fabric, cut:
2 strips, 1½" x 32½"
2 pieces, 1½" x 8½"
8 pieces, 1½" x 3¼"
4 binding strips, 2¼" x 42"

PIECING THE BACKGROUND

1. Place an ivory 9¼" square on top of each dark-purple 9¼" square, right sides together. Using a pencil and ruler, draw a diagonal line from corner to corner on the wrong side of the ivory square. Stitch a scant ¼" from both sides of the drawn line. Cut the square apart on the drawn line and press the seam allowances toward the dark triangles. Each pair of squares should yield two half-square-triangle units for a total of four. The squares should measure 8⅞" x 8⅞".

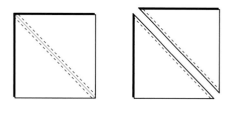

2. Place one unit from step 1 on top of another, with the light triangles facing the dark triangles and the seams aligned. Using a pencil and ruler, draw a diagonal line on the wrong side from corner to corner, perpendicular to the seam. Stitch a scant ¼" from both sides of the drawn line. Cut the square apart on the drawn line and press the seam allowances to one side. Repeat with the second pair of units. Each pair of units will yield two quarter-square-triangle units for a total of four. The squares should measure 8½" x 8½".

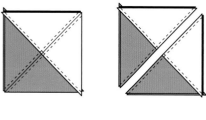

Make 4.

3. Stitch the four quarter-square-triangle units into a row as shown, with the dark background triangles adjacent to each other. Press the seam allowances in one direction.

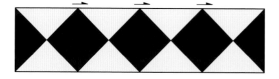

4. Stitch the purple 1½" x 32½" inner-border strips to the long edges of the pieced center. Press the seam allowances toward the inner-border strips.

APPLIQUÉING THE TABLE RUNNER

Refer to "The Appliqué Process" on page 12.

1. Use the pattern on pages 40 and 41 to make a complete pattern of the iris appliqué. Trace the complete pattern onto plastic or vinyl to make the overlay.

2. Use the pattern to make freezer-paper templates for the appliqués. Refer to the color key on page 39 to prepare the appliqués from the fabrics indicated.

3. Refer to the pattern and "Making Bias Strips and Stems" on page 18 to make stem pieces 2 and 7. Cut the pieces 1¼" wide for ¼"-wide finished stems.

4. Appliqué the following pieces together to make units: 11 and 12, 16 and 17, and 18 and 19.

5. Appliqué pieces 1–21 to one end of the background, stitching in numerical order.

6. Remove all freezer-paper templates.

7. Repeat steps 4–6 to appliqué a second iris on the other end of the background.

COMPLETING THE TABLE-RUNNER TOP

1. Stitch the floral print 3¼" x 32½" outer-border strips to the long edges of the quilt top. Press the seam allowances toward the inner-border strips.

2. Using two purple 1½" x 3¼" pieces, two floral print 1½" squares, and a purple 1½" x 8½" piece, sew a border row as shown. Press the seam allowances toward the purple pieces. Repeat to make a second

IRIS TABLE RUNNER

row. Stitch the rows to the short edges of the quilt top. Press the seam allowances toward the rows just added.

Make 2.

3. Using two floral print 3¼" squares, two purple 1½" x 3¼" pieces, and a floral print 3¼" x 8½" strip, sew a border row as shown. Press the seam allowances toward the purple pieces. Repeat to make a second border row.

Make 2.

4. Stitch the border rows to the short edges of the quilt top. Press the seam allowances toward the rows just added.

FINISHING

1. Layer the appliquéd top with batting and backing; baste the layers together.

2. Quilt as desired.

3. Refer to "Binding" on page 23 to finish your table runner.

COLOR KEY	
Fabric color	**Piece(s)**
Palest mauve	13
Very pale mauve	15, 19
Pale mauve	14, 18
Medium-dark mauve	11, 16
Dark mauve #1	12, 17, 21
Dark mauve #2	9
Gold	20
Light yellow-green	2, 7
Light green	4, 10
Medium green	5, 8
Medium-dark green	1, 3, 6

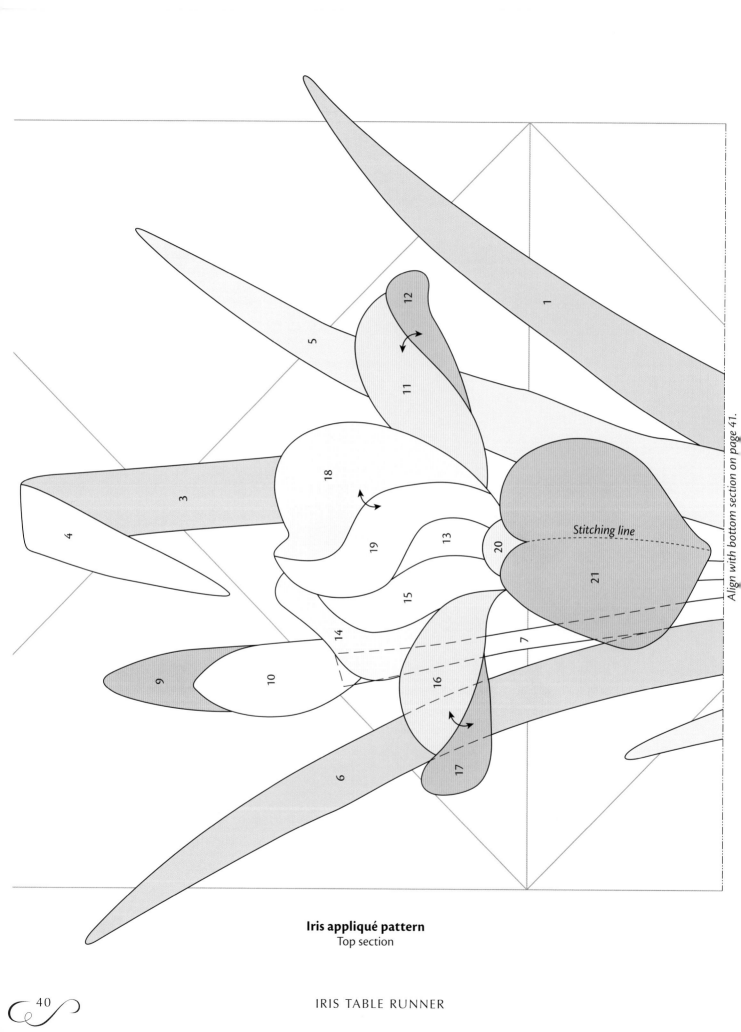

Iris appliqué pattern
Top section

Align with bottom section on page 41.

Stitching line

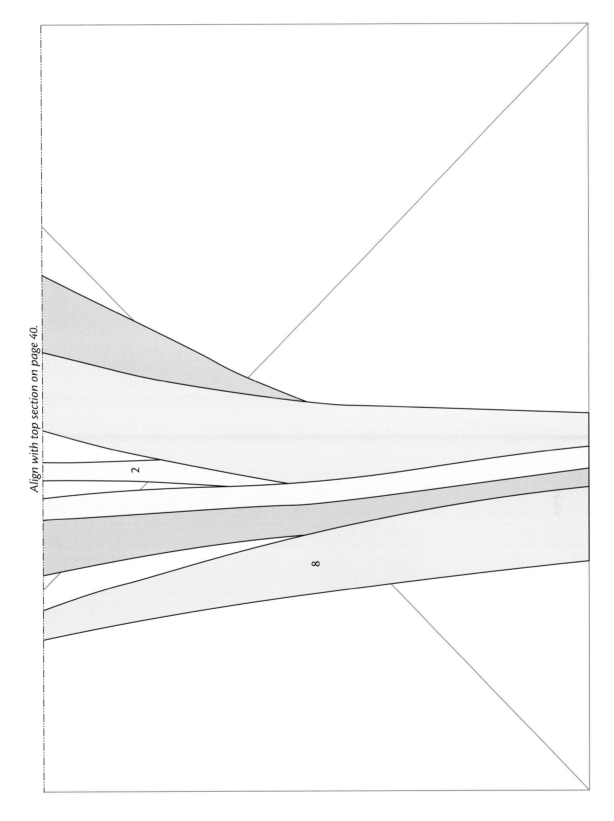

Align with top section on page 40.

2

8

Iris appliqué pattern
Bottom section

TULIP Place Mats

This place-mat design gives you an opportunity to use one of those amazing fabrics that you might have trouble finding a use for in a quilt. After I bought the bamboo-print batik, I wasn't quite sure what I wanted to do with it, but it works beautifully for the main fabric in these place mats. If you prefer, you can use a border print in place of the tulip appliqué. That diagonal swath is a great place to use up some shorter or leftover pieces of border fabric.

Finished size: 18" x 14"

MATERIALS FOR FOUR PLACE MATS

All yardages are based on 42"-wide fabric.

1 yard of print for main place-mat fabric

⅜ yard of contrasting print for appliqué background

1 fat quarter of dark-green fabric for contrasting strips

Scraps of at least 3 different green fabrics for leaves and stems

Scraps of at least 2 different red fabrics for tulip petals

Scraps of at least 2 different salmon-pink fabrics for tulip petals

⅝ yard of print fabric for binding

1¼ yards of fabric for backing

4 pieces of batting, 15" x 19" each*

Plastic or vinyl for overlay

Freezer paper

*To create a quilted look without making the place mat thick, I suggest Hobbs Thermore batting, which is extremely thin and lightweight.

CUTTING FOR FOUR PLACE MATS

All measurements include ¼"-wide seam allowances.

From the main fabric, cut:
4 rectangles, 14" x 18"

From the contrasting fabric, cut:
4 strips, 5½" x 17"

From the dark-green fabric, cut:
4 strips, 1" x 17"

4 strips, 1" x 7"

From the binding fabric, cut:
8 strips, 2¼" x 42"

PIECING THE PLACE MATS

1. Measure 11" from the upper-left corner along the top of a main-fabric 14" x 18" rectangle and make a mark. Measure 11" down the left side of the rectangle and make a mark. Align a rotary-cutting ruler with the marks as shown and cut, removing the upper-left corner of the rectangle.

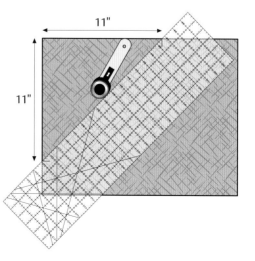

2. Make a mark 4¾" from the corner on each of the short sides of the triangle that was removed. Align the ruler with the marks as shown and cut, removing the smaller upper-left corner. Keep the small triangle and discard the center strip.

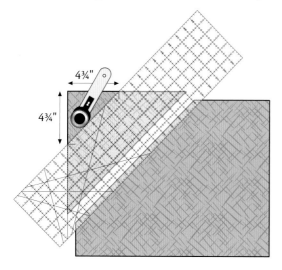

3. Press a dark-green 1" x 17" strip and a dark-green 1" x 7" strip in half lengthwise, wrong sides together.

4. With the raw edges aligned, center the dark-green 17" strip on the diagonal-cut corner of the larger fabric piece, right sides together, and baste in place by machine using a very scant ¼" seam allowance.

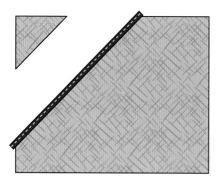

5. Center one edge of a contrasting 5½" x 17" piece with the diagonal edge of the main fabric, right sides together, and stitch. Press the seam allowances toward the main fabric.

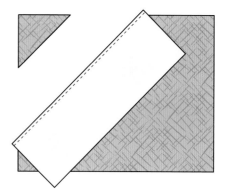

6. Using a rotary-cutting ruler, align the edge of the ruler with the top edge of the main fabric and trim the excess from the contrasting background and accent strip.

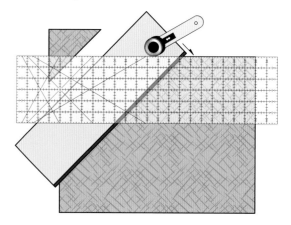

7. Align the edge of the ruler with the left edge of the main fabric and trim the excess from the contrasting background and accent strip.

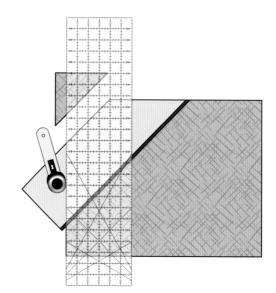

8. Center the pressed dark-green 7"-long strip on the upper-left diagonal of the contrasting background with raw edges aligned and baste in place by machine as before.

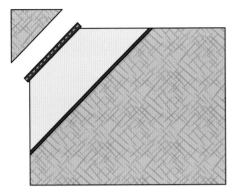

9. Place the long side of the 4¾" triangle on the upper-left diagonal of the contrasting background, right sides together. The accent strip will be sandwiched in between and there will be extra fabric on either end. Stitch along the diagonal; press the seam allowances toward the upper-left corner.

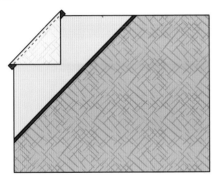

10. Align the edge of your ruler with the top edge of the main fabric and trim the excess from the upper-left corner.

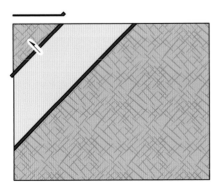

11. Align the edge of the ruler with the left edge of the main fabric and trim the excess from the upper-left corner. You should now have a 14" x 18" rectangle.

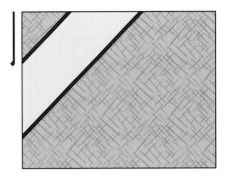

12. Repeat steps 1–11 to make three more place mats.

APPLIQUÉING THE PLACE MATS

Refer to "The Appliqué Process" on page 12.

1. Use the pattern on page 47 to make a complete pattern of the tulip appliqué. Trace the complete pattern onto plastic or vinyl to make the overlay.

2. Use the pattern to make freezer-paper templates for the appliqués. Refer to the color key on page 46 to prepare the appliqué from the fabrics indictaed.

3. Refer to "Making Bias Strips and Stems" on page 18 to make stem piece 3. Cut the strip 1¼" wide for a ¼"-wide finished stem.

4. Appliqué the following pieces together to make units: 1 and 2, and 9 and 10.

5. Appliqué pieces 1–10 to the background, stitching in numerical order.

6. Remove the freezer-paper templates.

7. Repeat steps 3–6 for the rest of the place mats.

FINISHING

1. Layer the appliquéd tops with batting and backing; baste the layers together.

2. Quilt as desired.

3. Refer to "Binding" on page 23 to finish your quilted place mats.

COLOR KEY	
Fabric color	**Piece(s)**
Light green	1
Medium green	2
Light yellow-green	3
Light salmon pink	4, 10
Medium salmon pink	5, 6
Red	7
Dark red	8, 9

A fussy-cut border print combines well with a whimsical large-scale print in the place mat.

Adding a satin fabric for the trim dresses up these Christmas place mats.

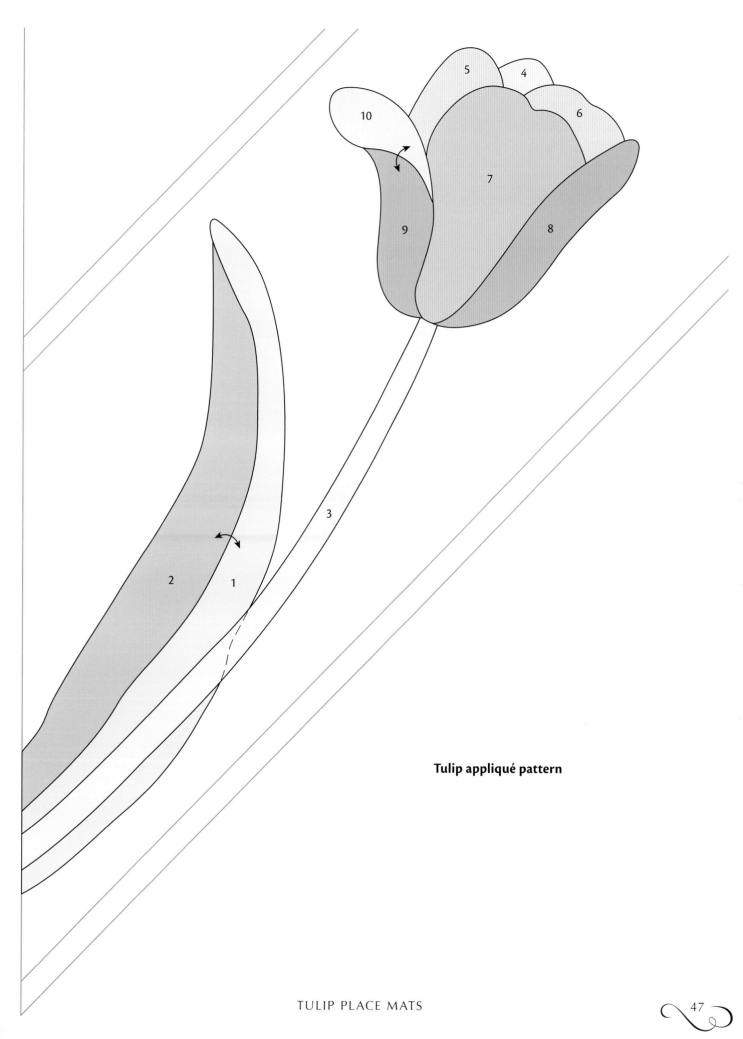

Tulip appliqué pattern

HOSTA Cushion

Hostas are beautiful plants, and we had a number of them growing in our garden in England. They grew quite well there, except for the fact that the snails and slugs loved to eat them. By the end of the summer the leaves would be turned to lace. Thinking of that when I designed this cushion, I decided to appliqué the hosta plant on top of Snail's Trail blocks. Here, the hosta plant has triumphed over the snails! I used tone-on-tone fabrics for the leaves, but if you have striped prints they would work well to mimic the lovely variegated varieties of hostas.

Finished size: 20" x 20"

MATERIALS

All yardages are based on 42"-wide fabric.

½ yard of light-taupe fabric for background blocks

1 fat quarter of medium-taupe fabric for background blocks

1 fat quarter of dark-taupe #1 fabric for background blocks

¼ yard of dark-taupe #2 fabric for piping

1 fat eighth *each* of 6 different green fabrics for leaves

Scraps of green fabric for stems

Scrap of very light-green fabric for leaves

22" x 22" square of muslin (⅝ yard) for backing

⅔ yard of fabric for cushion back

21" x 21" piece of batting

2½ yards of ¼" cording

20" zipper to match cushion back

20" square pillow form

Plastic or vinyl for overlay

Freezer paper

CUTTING

All measurements include ¼"-wide seam allowances. To make construction easy and avoid confusion, label your triangles as you cut them.

From the light-taupe fabric, cut:

8 squares, 1¾" x 1¾"

2 squares, 3¾" x 3¾"; cut twice diagonally to yield 8 quarter-square A triangles

4 squares, 3⅜" x 3⅜"; cut once diagonally to yield 8 half-square B triangles

2 squares, 6¼" x 6¼"; cut twice diagonally to yield 8 quarter-square C triangles

4 squares, 5⅞" x 5⅞"; cut once diagonally to yield 8 half-square D triangles

From the medium-taupe fabric, cut:

4 squares, 1¾" x 1¾"

1 square, 3¾" x 3¾"; cut twice diagonally to yield 4 quarter-square A triangles

2 squares, 3⅜" x 3⅜"; cut once diagonally to yield 4 half-square B triangles

1 square, 6¼" x 6¼"; cut twice diagonally to yield 4 quarter-square C triangles

2 squares, 5⅞" x 5⅞"; cut once diagonally to yield 4 half-square D triangles

(Continued on page 50)

HOSTA CUSHION

From the dark-taupe #1 fabric, cut:

4 squares, 1¾" x 1¾"

1 square, 3¾" x 3¾"; cut twice diagonally to yield 4 quarter-square A triangles

2 squares, 3⅜" x 3⅜"; cut once diagonally to yield 4 half-square B triangles

1 square, 6¼" x 6¼"; cut twice diagonally to yield 4 quarter-square C triangles

2 squares, 5⅞" x 5⅞"; cut once diagonally to yield 4 half-square D triangles

From the dark-taupe #2 fabric, cut:

3 strips, 1¼" x 42"

From the cushion back fabric, cut:

2 rectangles, 11½" x 21"

PIECING THE CUSHION TOP

1. Arrange two light-taupe, one medium-taupe, and one dark-taupe 1¾" square to form a four-patch unit. Stitch and press the seam allowances toward the darker fabrics.

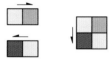

2. Stitch a medium-taupe A triangle to the top of the four-patch unit and a dark-taupe A triangle to the bottom as shown. Press the seam allowances away from the center. Stitch light-taupe A triangles to both sides of the center square. Press the seam allowances away from the center.

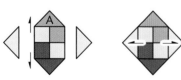

3. Stitch light-taupe B triangles to the upper-right and lower-left sides of the unit from step 2 as shown. Press the seam allowances away from the center. Stitch a medium-taupe B triangle to the upper-left side and a dark-taupe B triangle to the lower-right side. Press away from the center. The square should measure 5½" x 5½".

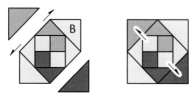

4. Stitch light-taupe C triangles to the top and bottom of the square as shown. Press the seam allowances away from the center. Stitch a dark-taupe C triangle to the right side of the square and a medium-taupe C triangle to the left side of the square. Press away from the center.

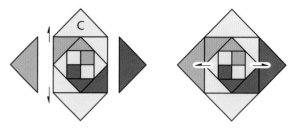

5. Stitch a dark-taupe D triangle to the upper-right side and a medium-taupe D triangle to the lower-left side of the square as shown. Press the seam allowances away from the center. Stitch light-taupe D triangles to the upper-left and lower-right sides. Press away from the center. The block should measure 10½" x 10½".

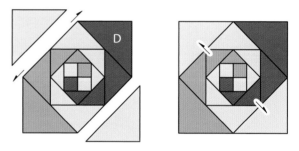

6. Repeat steps 1–5 to make a total of four blocks.

7. Arrange the four blocks into two rows as shown, with the dark D triangles toward the center and the medium D triangles in the corners. Sew the blocks into rows. Press the seam allowances open. Sew the rows together, matching the seams. Press the seam allowances open.

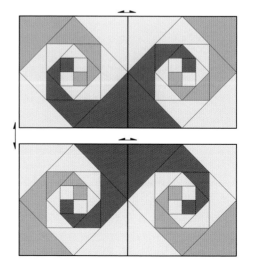

APPLIQUÉING THE CUSHION

Refer to "The Appliqué Process" on page 12.

1. Use the pattern on pages 52–55 to make a complete pattern of the hosta appliqué. Trace the complete pattern onto plastic or vinyl to make the overlay. Position the overlay onto the pieced background, roughly centering the hosta with the center of the background.

2. Use the pattern to make freezer-paper templates for the appliqués. Refer to the color key, below right, to prepare the appliqués from the fabrics indicated.

3. Refer to the pattern and "Making Bias Strips and Stems" on page 18 to make stem pieces 1–9. Cut the bias strips 1¼" wide for ¼"-wide finished stems.

4. Appliqué the following pieces together to make units: 10 and 11, 12 and 13, 14 and 15, 16 and 17, 18 and 19, 20 and 21, 22 and 23, 24 and 25, 26 and 27, 28 and 29, 30 and 31, 32 and 33, 34 and 35, 36 and 37, 38 and 39, 40 and 41, 42–44, 45 and 46, 47 and 48, and 49 and 50.

5. Appliqué pieces 1–50 to the background, stitching in numerical order.

Appliqué placement guide

6. Remove all freezer-paper templates.

FINISHING

1. Layer the appliquéd top with batting and the muslin 22" square backing; baste the layers together.

2. Quilt as desired.

3. Refer to "Installing a Zipper" on page 24 for instructions on installing the zipper in the fabric for the cushion back. Install the zipper between the 21" sides of the two 11½" x 21" rectangles.

4. Refer to "Adding Piping" on page 25 to add the dark taupe piping to the edges of the cushion.

5. Partially open the zipper. Lay the back over the cushion front, right sides together. Pin, starting in the middle of the sides and working toward the corners. Stitch around the cushion using a ¼" seam allowance. Use a piping foot to stitch close to the piping, or stitch just to the outside of the piping with a zipper foot. After stitching, trim any excess fabric in the seam allowances and trim the corners at an angle.

6. Turn the pillow cover to the right side and insert the pillow form through the opening.

COLOR KEY	
Fabric color	**Piece(s)**
Very light green	43
Light-green #1	32, 39, 42, 45, 48, 50
Light-green #2	33, 38, 44, 46, 47, 49
Medium-green #1	12, 14, 24, 30, 35, 36, 40
Medium-green #2	13, 15, 25, 31, 34, 37, 41
Dark-green #1	11, 16, 18, 20, 22, 27, 28
Dark-green #2	10, 17, 19, 21, 23, 26, 29
Green fabric for stems	1–9

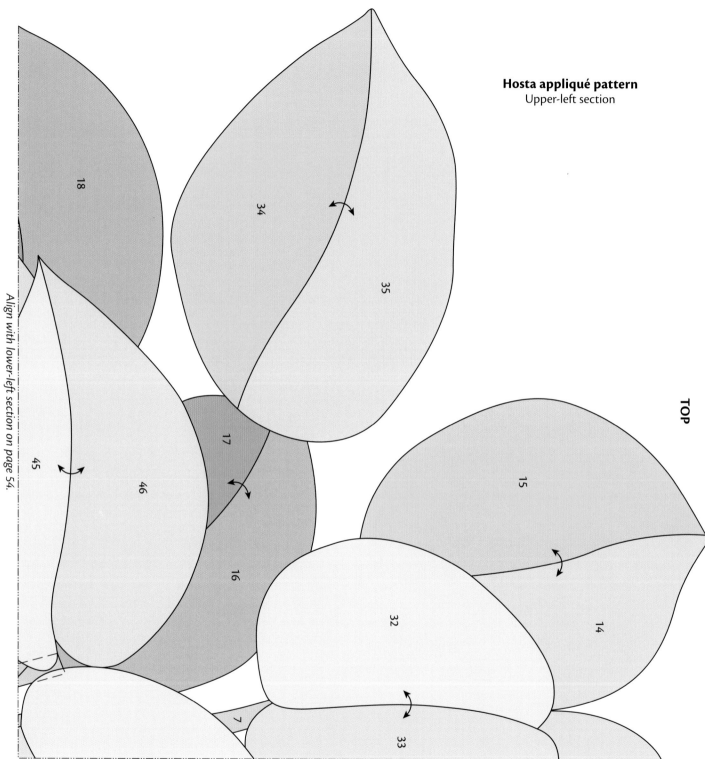

Hosta appliqué pattern
Upper-left section

TOP

18

34

35

17

46

45

16

15

32

14

7

33

Align with lower-left section on page 54.

Align with upper-right section on page 53.

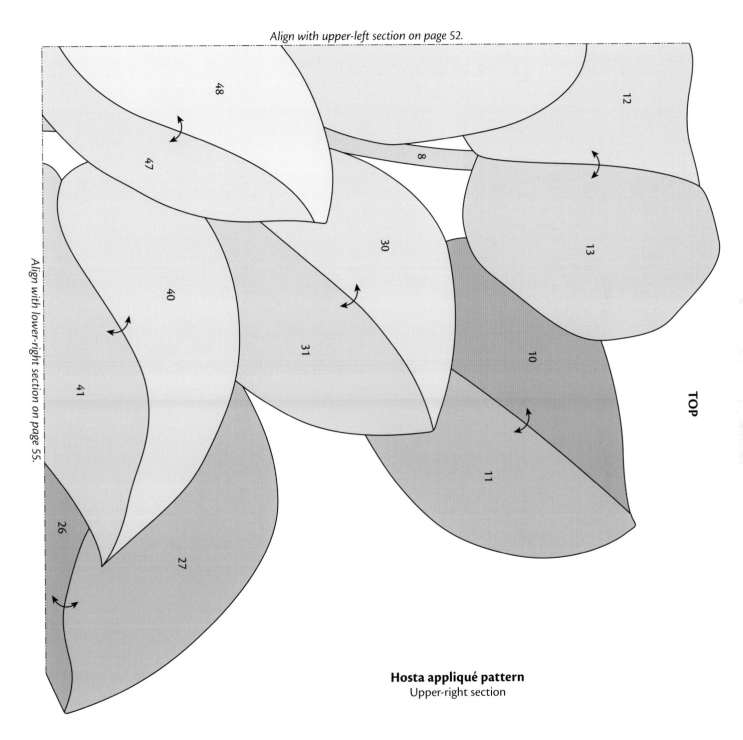

Align with upper-left section on page 52.

Align with lower-right section on page 55.

48

12

47

8

30

13

40

31

10

41

11

26

27

TOP

Hosta appliqué pattern
Upper-right section

Hosta appliqué pattern
Lower-left section

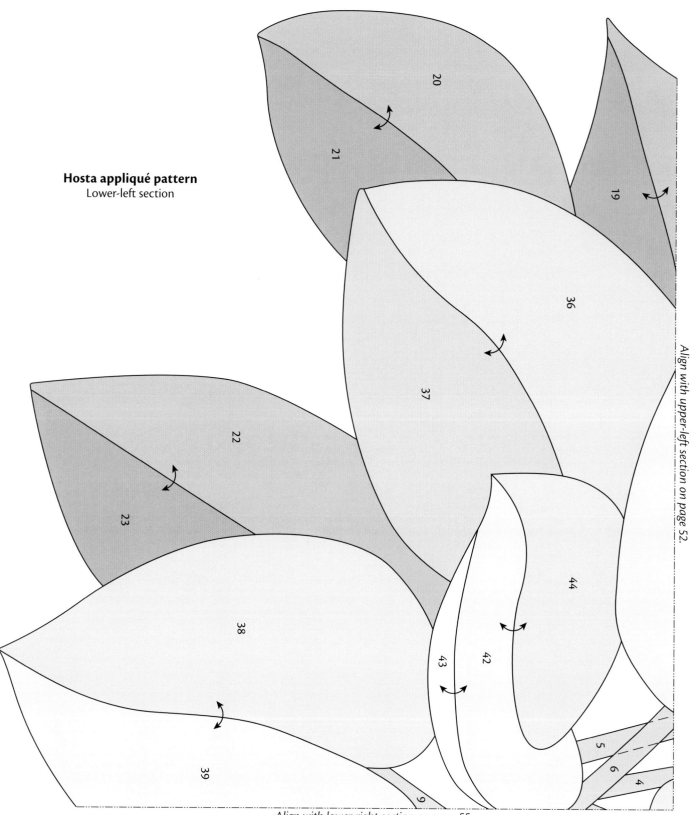

Align with upper-left section on page 52.

Align with lower-right section on page 55.

HOSTA CUSHION

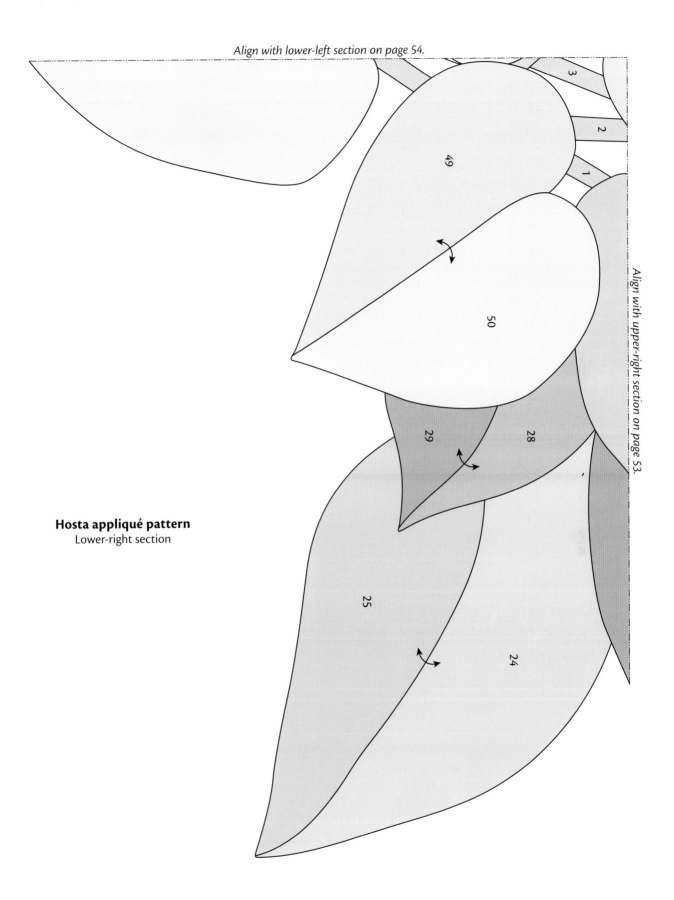

Hosta appliqué pattern
Lower-right section

Align with upper-right section on page 53.

CAMPANULA Neck Roll

After making many square and round cushions for my other books, I thought it would be fun to make a neck-roll cushion. The dainty campanula flowers fit very nicely in this design. This cushion has a little story: Just after I moved back to the United States, the quilting group I belonged to in England, the Yorkshire Yanks, sent me a piece of floral fabric as a challenge. The fabric worked very well with the color of the flowers, and I used it on the ends of this lovely cushion.

Finished size: 15" x 6"

MATERIALS

All yardages are based on 42"-wide fabric.

½ yard of green fabric for contrasting strips and piping

⅓ yard of floral print for borders and ends

1 fat quarter of pale-green print for appliqué background

Scraps of 3 different purple fabrics for flowers

Scraps of 3 different pinkish-purple fabrics for flowers

Scraps of 4 different green fabrics for leaves

17½" x 21" piece of muslin for backing

16½" x 19" piece of batting

1⅓ yards of ¼" cording

12" zipper to match floral fabric

6" x 15" neck-roll pillow form*

Plastic or vinyl for overlay

Freezer paper

See "Size Variations" at right if you can't find this size.

Size Variations

Neck-roll cushions come in a wide variety of sizes. For this project, I used an insert 15" long and 6" in diameter. If you're unable to find a ready-made insert this size, you can eliminate the zipper and simply stuff the cushion with fiberfill; then slip-stitch the seam when you're finished. There are some inserts available in fabric stores that measure 6" x 18". If you find an insert this size, you can simply cut the floral print a little wider by adding half of the extra length to the measurement of each rectangle. For the 6" x 18" inserts, cut the floral print rectangles 5¼" x 20¼" (3¾" + 1½" = 5¼").

CUTTING

All measurements include seam allowances.

From the floral print, cut:
2 rectangles, 3¾" x 20¼"

2 circles, 6½" diameter, using template (page 61)

From the pale-green print, cut:
1 rectangle, 10" x 21"

From the green fabric, cut:
2 strips, 1" x 20¼"

2 strips, 1¼" x 22", cut on the bias

APPLIQUÉING THE NECK ROLL

Refer to "The Appliqué Process" on page 12.

1. Use the pattern on page 60 to make a complete pattern of the floral appliqué. Use appliqué pieces 1–55. Trace the complete pattern onto plastic or vinyl to make the overlay.

2. Use the pattern to make freezer-paper templates for the appliqués. Refer to the color key on page 59 to prepare the appliqués from the fabrics indicated.

3. Appliqué the following pieces together to make units for the leaves: 1 and 2, 3 and 4, 7 and 8, 9 and 10, 11 and 12, 13 and 14, 15 and 16, 18 and 19, 20 and 21, 22 and 23, and 24 and 25.

4. Appliqué pieces 1–55 to the pale-green print rectangle, stitching in numerical order.

5. Remove all freezer-paper templates.

6. Trim the appliquéd rectangle so that it measures 9" x 20¼".

ASSEMBLING THE NECK ROLL

1. Press each green 1" x 20¼" strip in half lengthwise, wrong sides together. With the raw edges aligned and using a very scant ¼" seam allowance, baste a strip to one long edge of both floral print 3¾" x 20¼" rectangles.

2. Stitch the step 1 rectangles to opposite sides of the appliquéd rectangle as shown, right sides together. The contrasting strip should be next to the appliquéd rectangle. Press the seam allowances toward the center.

FINISHING

1. Layer the appliquéd top with batting and the muslin backing, centering the appliquéd top on the batting, right side up. The batting should be ⅝" inside each of the short edges to minimize bulk when the zipper is installed, but it should extend past the long edges. Baste the layers together.

2. Quilt as desired. Trim the extra batting and backing fabric; the rectangle should measure 15½" x 20¼". Baste the layers together a scant ¼" from each of the short edges.

3. With right sides together, pin the 15½" edges of the cushion top, matching seams. Using a ⅝" seam allowance, stitch the first 1¾" on either end with a normal-length stitch, backstitching on both ends of the seams. Then stitch the remaining seam with a longer basting stitch. Press the seam allowances open.

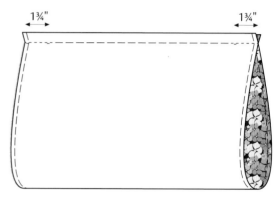

4. Refer to "Installing a Zipper" on page 24 for instructions on installing the zipper. If you'd like both ends to be reinforced, follow the instructions for adding reinforcement tabs on both ends of the zipper. The zipper slider should just meet the regular stitching and tab on one end and the zipper stop should be at or past the regular stitching and tab on the other end. It will be a little tricky to topstitch the zipper to the tube. You may need to remove the platform from your sewing machine if you have a machine with a free arm. Or you can

sew half the zipper from one direction, remove it, and stitch the other half from the opposite side. Unzip the zipper and leave it open.

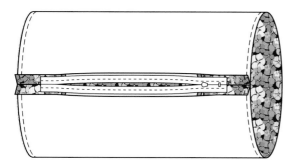

5. Refer to "Adding Piping" on page 25 for instructions on making and adding piping to a round cushion, using the green 1¼" x 22" bias strips. Baste the piping to both floral print circles.

6. Fold both circles in half and finger-press. Then fold the tube in half and finger-press. With right sides together, pin the raw edges of one end of the quilted tube around one piped circle, lining up the finger folds of the circle with the finger folds on the tube and easing the fabric to fit. Baste the pieces together, following the basting lines on the piping. If you don't have a piping foot, you might find it easier to baste by hand. Then repeat with the other end.

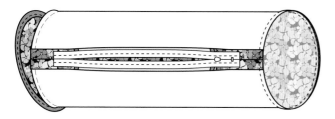

7. Using a ¼" seam allowance and a zipper or piping foot, stitch around the circles. Turn the cushion cover to the right side through the zipper opening and insert the pillow form.

A large-scale print or even a border print can be used for the center panel of the neck roll.

COLOR KEY	
Fabric color	**Piece(s)**
Pale purple	39, 47, 48, 49
Light purple	28, 29, 30, 38, 40, 46, 50
Purple	26, 27, 36, 37
Pale pinkish purple	34, 35, 45, 53, 55
Light pinkish purple	32, 33, 44, 51, 52, 54
Pinkish purple	31, 41, 42, 43
Medium-light green	2, 7, 9, 12, 14, 16, 17, 19, 20, 23
Medium-green #1	1, 10, 15, 21, 22
Medium-green #2	3, 5, 8, 11, 13, 18, 25
Dark green	4, 6, 24

Campanula appliqué pattern

TOP

6½" circle

DAFFODIL Tote Bag

This bag is a fabulous way to show off your appliqué skills and it's just the right size for carrying books. The bag features one outside pocket and one inside pocket, but you can choose to add more or fewer. The outside pocket is large enough to hold a quilt book or large pattern. Use any weight of interfacing or batting to determine how soft or rigid you'd like your bag to be. This pattern also works for many of the preprinted fabric panels or for an orphan block. Add borders as necessary to make any smaller block work; the front of the bag just needs to measure 14½" x 16½" before stitching.

Finished size: 14" x 16" x 4"

MATERIALS

All yardages are based on 42"-wide fabric.

1 yard of print fabric for lining

½ yard of dark-blue #1 fabric for sides, bottom, and handles

⅜ yard of blue print #1 for back and pockets

⅓ yard of blue print #2 for front and back borders

1 fat eighth of light-blue print for front background

⅛ yard of dark-blue #2 fabric for narrow border

Scraps of 6 different yellow to orange fabrics for flowers

Scraps of 5 different green fabrics for leaves and stems

Scrap of grayish-green fabric for calyx (flower base)

18½" x 36½" piece of fusible interfacing or fusible batting

10½" x 12½" piece of fusible interfacing

2 pieces of interfacing or batting, 1" x 18"

Plastic or vinyl for overlay

Freezer paper

CUTTING

All measurements include ¼"-wide seam allowances unless otherwise noted.

From the light-blue print, cut:
1 rectangle, 7½" x 9½"

From the dark-blue #2 fabric, cut:
4 strips, 1½" x 9½"

From the blue print #2, cut:
2 strips, 3" x 9½"
2 strips, 3" x 16½"
2 strips, 2½" x 10½"
2 strips, 2½" x 16½"

From the blue print #1, cut:
1 center back, 10½" x 12½"
1 outside pocket, 10½" x 12½"
1 inside pocket, 8½" x 9½"

From the lining fabric, cut:
1 bag lining, 18½" x 36½"
1 outside-pocket lining, 10½" x 12½"
1 inside-pocket lining, 8½" x 9½"

From the dark-blue #1 fabric, cut:
4 side pieces, 2½" x 16½"
1 bottom piece, 4½" x 18½"
2 handle pieces, 4" x 17"

CONSTRUCTING THE APPLIQUÉ FRONT

Refer to "The Appliqué Process" on page 12.

1. Use the pattern on page 68 to make a complete pattern of the floral appliqué. Trace the complete pattern onto plastic or vinyl to make the overlay.

2. Use the pattern to make freezer-paper templates for the appliqués. Refer to the color key on page 67 to prepare the appliqués from the fabrics indicated.

3. Sew dark-blue 1½" x 9½" border strips to the sides of the light-blue 7½" x 9½" background rectangle. Press seam allowances toward the border. Sew a dark-blue 1½" x 9½" strip to the top only. Press.

4. Appliqué the following pieces together to make units: 20 and 21, 30 and 31, and 38 and 39.

5. Appliqué pieces 1–6 to the background, stitching in numerical order. Baste the lower end of piece 7 in place. Appliqué pieces 8–16 to the background, stitching in numerical order. Appliqué pieces 7 and 17–41, stitching in numerical order.

6. Add the remaining dark-blue 1½" x 9½" border strip to the bottom of the background rectangle. Press. Then add the blue print 3" x 9½" strips to the top and bottom and press away from the center. Add the blue print 3" x 16½" strips to the sides. Press.

7. Remove all freezer-paper templates.

Back of "Daffodil Tote Bag"

CONSTRUCTING THE BAG EXTERIOR

1. Following the manufacturer's instructions, fuse the 10½" x 12½" fusible-interfacing piece to the wrong side of the blue print 10½" x 12½" rectangle for the outside pocket.

2. Place the outside pocket and outside-pocket lining 10½" x 12½" rectangle right sides together. Stitch along the top. Turn to the right side and press flat. Topstitch ¼" from the seam.

3. Add one blue print 2½" x 10½" border strip to the top of the blue print 10½" x 12½" center-back piece. Press the seam allowances away from the center. Position the pocket so that the bottom raw edges align with the raw edge of the center back and the pocket lining is facing the right side of the center back. Baste the side and bottom raw edges together.

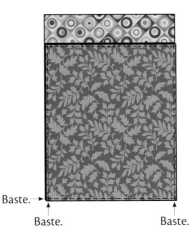

Baste.→
Baste.   Baste.

4. Add the remaining blue print 2½" x 10½" border strip to the bottom of the center back, and then add the blue print 2½" x 16½" border strips to the sides.

5. Stitch dark-blue 2½" x 16½" side pieces to the left and right of the bag front. Then stitch the remaining dark-blue 2½" x 16½" side pieces to the left and right of the bag back. Press seam allowances toward the dark blue.

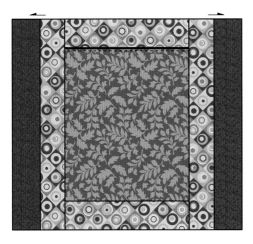

6. Stitch the dark-blue 4½" x 18½" strip to the bottom of both the back and front of the bag. Press toward the dark-blue strip.

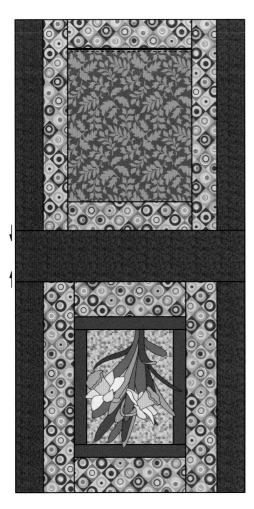

7. Following the manufacturer's instructions, fuse the 18½" x 36½" piece of interfacing or batting to the wrong side of the pieced bag. Topstitch or quilt as desired, but do not stitch on the pocket.

8. Fold the bag in half, right sides together, and line up the top edges. Stitch along both sides.

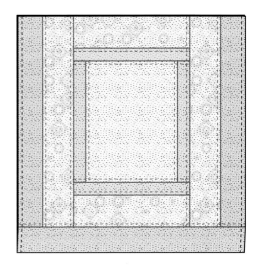

9. Refer to "Making Boxed Corners" on page 26 to form the corners at the bottom of the bag. The distance from the point to the marked line should be 2" and the corner seam should be 4" long.

CONSTRUCTING THE LINING

1. On each of the blue print #1 and lining fabric 8½" x 9½" pieces for the inside pocket, fold one 8½" side over ¼" to the wrong side and press. This will be the bottom of the pocket.

2. Place the inside pocket and inside-pocket lining right sides together. Stitch along the three sides that are not folded. Clip close to the top corners. Turn right side out and press flat. Topstitch ¼" from the seam along the top only.

3. Position the pocket onto the lining fabric 18½" x 36½" piece with the pocket lining facing the right side of the lining. Center the pocket, with the top of the pocket 2½" from one short edge of the lining. Pin in place. Stitch around the sides and bottom of the pocket ⅛" from the edges.

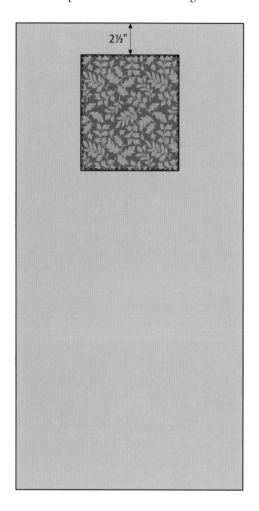

4. Fold the lining in half, right sides together, and align the top edges. Stitch along one side completely. On the other side, stitch the bottom 5", and then leave an opening about 6" long and resume stitching to the top.

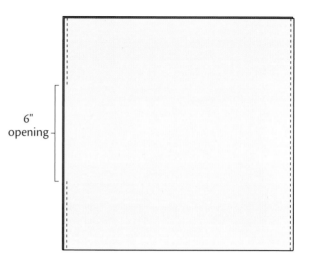

5. Repeat step 9 of "Constructing the Bag Exterior" on page 65 to form two corners at the bottom of the lining. The distance from the point to the marked line should be 2" and the corner seam should be 4" long.

FINISHING THE BAG

1. Refer to "Making Bag Handles" on page 27 for instructions on making the handles.

2. On the front of the bag, position one end of a handle, right sides together, aligned with the vertical seam line as shown and with the raw edges of the handle extending ¼" above the raw edges of the bag. Baste in place. Position the other end of the handle so that it's aligned with the other vertical seam

and with the raw edges of the handle extending ¼" above the raw edges of the bag. Make sure that the handle is not twisted. Baste in place.

3. Repeat step 2 with the second handle on the back of the bag.

4. Turn the lining inside out and slip the bag inside the lining so that the right side of the bag faces the right side of the lining. Pin the raw edges of the tops together, matching the side seams. Stitch around the top using a ¼" seam allowance.

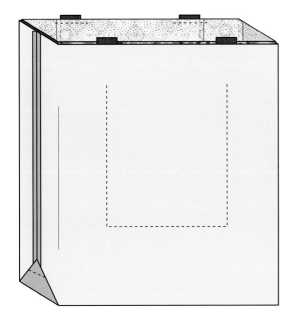

5. Reach in through the side opening in the lining and turn the bag right side out. Press the top seam flat. Topstitch ¼" from the top edge.

6. Hand stitch the opening in the lining closed or fold each edge under ¼" and stitch close to the folds by machine.

Secure the Lining

To keep the lining from coming out of the bag, before the side opening is stitched closed, I stitch the bottom inside corner triangle of the lining and the bag together, just outside the seam line.

COLOR KEY	
Fabric color	**Piece(s)**
Pale green	7, 15, 21, 23
Light green	2, 6, 9, 14, 17
Medium green	1, 8, 11, 13, 16, 19
Dark green	3, 5, 18, 20
Dark blue-green	4, 10, 12
Gray-green	22, 24
Pale yellow	26, 32, 36, 40
Light yellow	28, 33, 41
Light orange-yellow	25, 27, 34, 35
Orange-yellow	29, 37
Orange #1	30, 38
Orange #2	31, 39

Daffodil appliqué pattern

DAFFODIL TOTE BAG

This tote is made with a preprinted panel on the front in place of the daffodil appliqué.

DAHLIA Tote Bag

I love large tote bags because you can use them for so many things. I like to use them to carry quilts in progress or other projects. I designed this bag to be sturdy and roomy, but attractive as well! I used a single fabric with radiating lines that was perfect for all of the flower petals. I designed the floral appliqué from a photograph and didn't know what the flower was. I finally thought to ask my friend Chris Marne, who knows way more about plants than I do. Right away she told me it was a dahlia, which surprised me because I always think of the dahlia with the tightly packed petals. I've simplified it, but regardless, it's a fun flower to stitch.

Finished size: 13½" x 17¼" x 8"

MATERIALS

All yardages are based on 42"-wide fabric.

⅞ yard of dark-olive batik for straps

¾ yard of olive batik for front and back center, pocket, and binding

½ yard of taupe batik for bag bottom and binding

1 fat quarter of print fabric for pocket lining

1 fat quarter of yellow fabric for flower petals

⅛ yard *each* of 7 different batiks for pieced sides

Scraps of 9 different green fabrics for leaves and stems*

Scrap of brown speckled fabric for flower centers

22" x 42½" piece of print fabric for lining

23" x 45" piece of batting

2 pieces of interfacing or batting, 1½" x 67"

Plastic or vinyl for overlay

Freezer paper

Refer to the color key on page 76 for the range of greens.

CUTTING

All measurements include ¼"-wide seam allowances unless otherwise noted.

From the olive batik, cut:

2 rectangles, 12" x 14½", for front and back center

1 rectangle, 12" x 12½", for pocket

2 strips, 2¼" x 12", for binding

From the taupe batik, cut:

1 rectangle, 7¾" x 12", for bottom

1 rectangle, 7¾" x 32", for bottom

2 strips, 2¼" x 10½", for binding

From *each of 5* of the different batiks for pieced sides, cut:

1 strip, 2¾" x 42" (5 total)

From the 6th batik, cut:

1 square, 4" x 4"; cut in half diagonally to make 2 triangles

From the 7th batik, cut:

2 squares, 3½" x 3½"; cut in half diagonally to make 4 triangles

From the pocket lining fabric, cut:

1 rectangle, 12" x 12½"

From the dark-olive batik, cut:

4 strips, 6" x 38", for handles

APPLIQUÉING THE FRONT

Refer to "The Appliqué Process" on page 12.

1. Use the pattern on pages 80 and 81 to make a complete pattern of the floral appliqué. Use appliqué pieces 1–49. Trace the complete pattern onto plastic or vinyl to make the overlay.

2. Use the pattern to make freezer-paper templates for the appliqués. Refer to the color key on page 76 to prepare the appliqués from the fabrics indicated.

3. Appliqué the following pieces together to make units: 7 and 8, 9 and 10, 11 and 12, 15 and 16, 17 and 18, 19 and 20, and 21 and 22.

4. Refer to the pattern and "Making Bias Strips and Stems" on page 18 to make stem pieces 1–6. Cut the pieces 1¼" wide for ¼"-wide finished stems.

5. Stitch the taupe batik 7¾" x 12" rectangle for the bottom to the olive batik center-front background fabric. Press the seam allowances toward the taupe.

6. Appliqué pieces 1–49 to the background, stitching in numerical order.

Appliqué placement guide

7. Remove all freezer-paper templates.

CONSTRUCTING THE BAG SIDES

1. Use the patterns on pages 78 and 79 to make a complete pattern for the paper-foundation-pieced sides. Trace the pattern onto the dull side of freezer paper. It's not necessary to reverse the pattern. The marked side of the paper will be your guide for placing fabric; you'll place the fabric on the shiny side of the paper.

2. For piece number 1, use one of the triangles cut from the 4" square. With the fabric wrong side against the shiny side of the freezer paper, lay the triangle so that it's centered under piece 1 on the pattern and has at least ¼" of seam allowance on all three edges. You can hold the pattern up to the light if necessary to see the lines better. Pin the piece in place.

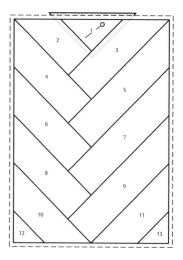

3. Fold the foundation paper back along the line between pieces 1 and 2. Trim the exposed piece 1 fabric ¼" from the folded paper.

4. Lay the long edge of a 2¾" x 42" strip of fabric that you want to be piece 2 along the trimmed edge of piece 1 with right sides together. The fabric strip should extend at least ¼" beyond all of the edges of piece 2. Pin in place through the folded freezer paper.

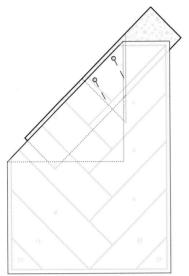

5. Stitch next to the fold in the freezer paper, beginning and ending at least ¼" before and after the line.

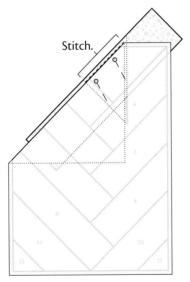

6. Unfold the freezer paper, and then fold the piece 2 fabric into place, making sure that it extends at least ¼" beyond the piece 2 lines. Press it in place against the freezer paper and trim away the excess strip, leaving at least a ¼" seam allowance around the entire piece.

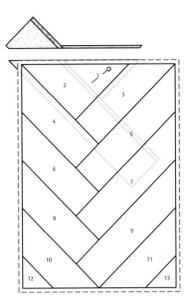

7. Using the same fabric strip for piece 3, continue in this manner to add the next piece, following the pattern for fabric placement. Use a second fabric strip for pieces 4 and 5, a third strip for pieces 6 and 7, a fourth strip for pieces 8 and 9, and the fifth strip for pieces 10 and 11. Use the triangles cut from 3½" squares for pieces 12 and 13. When the piecing is complete, trim the seam allowances around the outer edges of the rectangle to ¼". The rectangle should measure 10½" x 14½".

8. Gently remove the freezer paper.

9. Repeat steps 2–8 to make another pieced side, reusing the freezer-paper pattern.

CONSTRUCTING THE OUTER BAG

1. Place the olive batik 12" x 12½" pocket piece right sides together with the pocket lining fabric. Stitch along the 12" side. Fold right sides out and press flat. Topstitch ¼" from the seam.

2. Position the pocket so that the bottom raw edges align with the raw edge of the olive batik 12" x 14½" center-back piece and so that the pocket lining faces the right side of the center back. Baste the side and bottom raw edges together using a scant ¼" seam allowance.

3. Stitch a pieced side unit to each side of the center back, with right sides together. Press the seam allowances toward the center back.

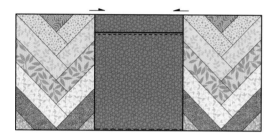

4. Stitch the taupe batik 7¾" x 32" rectangle to the bottom of the unit. Press toward the bottom.

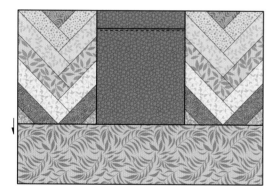

5. Stitch the appliquéd front to the right side of the unit, right sides together and matching the seams of the bottom fabric. Press toward the appliquéd section.

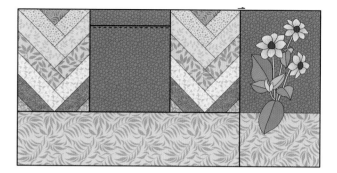

6. Layer the bag unit with batting, centering the bag right side up on the batting. Baste the layers together.

7. Quilt as desired. Trim the extra batting and stitch a scant ¼" seam along each edge if you've not already basted the edges.

8. Stitch the left side to the right of the front, matching the seams of the bottom fabric.

ADDING THE HANDLES

1. Place the end of one dark-olive handle strip perpendicular across the end of another strip, right sides together. Mark a diagonal line and stitch. Trim to a ¼" seam allowance and press the seam allowances open. Repeat with a second pair of strips. Trim each handle so that it measures 67" long.

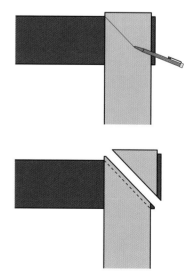

2. Refer to "Making Bag Handles" on page 27 for instructions on folding and stitching the bag handles. Use the 1½" x 67" strips of interfacing or batting to reinforce the handles.

3. Place a handle over one of the seams where the side meets the back, with the raw edge of the handle aligned with the bottom of the bag. The handle should overlap only ¼" on the foundation-pieced side and about 1¼" on the back panel. I didn't center the handle over the seam because I wanted more of the sides to be visible. You can center the handles over the seam if you prefer. Pin in place. Topstitch about ⅛" from both long edges, starting at the bottom and finishing about 1" from the top. Center the other end of the handle over the other side/back seam, making sure that the handle isn't twisted. Pin in place and topstitch.

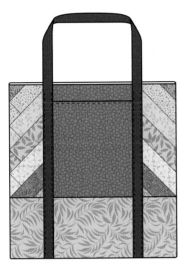

4. Repeat step 3 with the second handle centered over the side/front seams. Make sure that the handles will meet at the bottom.

5. Turn the bag inside out and with right sides together, pin the bottom of the bag, matching the center front with the center back and the front handle bottoms with the back handle bottoms. Stitch using a ½" seam allowance.

6. Refer to "Making Boxed Corners" on page 26 to form the two square corners at the bottom of the bag. The distance from the point to the marked line should be 4" and the corner seam should be 8" long.

FINISHING THE BAG

1. Fold the lining fabric in half, right sides together, and stitch both sides.

2. Repeat step 6 of "Adding the Handles," above, to form the two square corners at the bottom of the lining.

3. Place the lining inside the outer bag, wrong sides together. Match the side seams of the lining with the middle of the sides of the outer bag. Pin together along the top, making sure the handles are folded down out of the way. Baste together.

4. Piece a continuous binding strip, alternating the 2¼"-wide strips of olive batik and taupe batik and using a straight seam and ¼" seam allowance. Press the seam allowances open. Fold the strip in half lengthwise, wrong sides together, and press.

5. With raw edges aligned, place the binding strip around the outside top of the bag, aligning the seams of the binding with the seams of the outer bag. Make sure the handles are out of the way and stitch the binding to the bag using a ¼" seam allowance. Fold the binding to the inside of the bag and blindstitch it in place by hand.

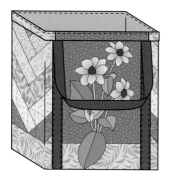

6. Pull the straps up and over the binding and pin in place. Stitch a 1¼" square to attach the straps to the binding. For extra reinforcement, stitch an X inside the stitched square.

COLOR KEY	
Fabric color	**Piece(s)**
Light yellow-green	13
Yellow-green	1–5
Pale green	6, 14
Light-green #1	12, 19
Light-green #2	11
Medium-green #1	10, 15, 22
Medium-green #2	8, 9, 16, 17, 21
Medium-green #3	7, 18
Medium-dark green	20
Yellow	23–30, 32–39, 41–48
Brown speckled	31, 40, 49

DAHLIA TOTE BAG

A wonderful preprinted batik panel is another option for the front or back panels.

DAHLIA TOTE BAG

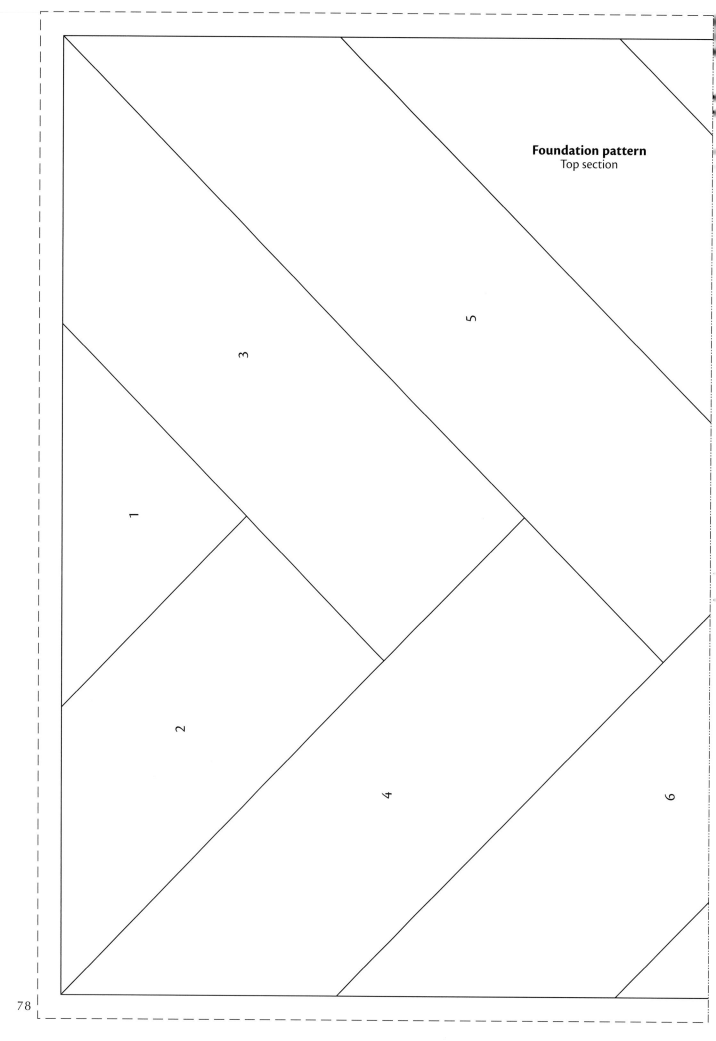

Foundation pattern
Top section

1

2

3

4

5

6

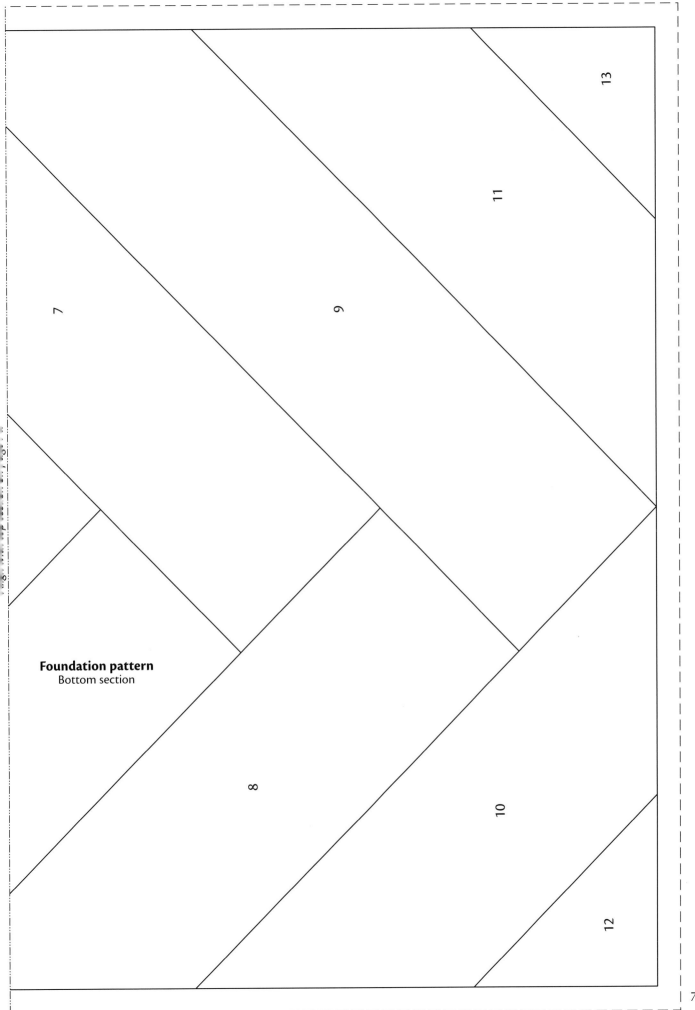

Foundation pattern
Bottom section

Dahlia appliqué pattern
Top section

Align with bottom section on page 81.

DAHLIA TOTE BAG

Align with top section on page 80.

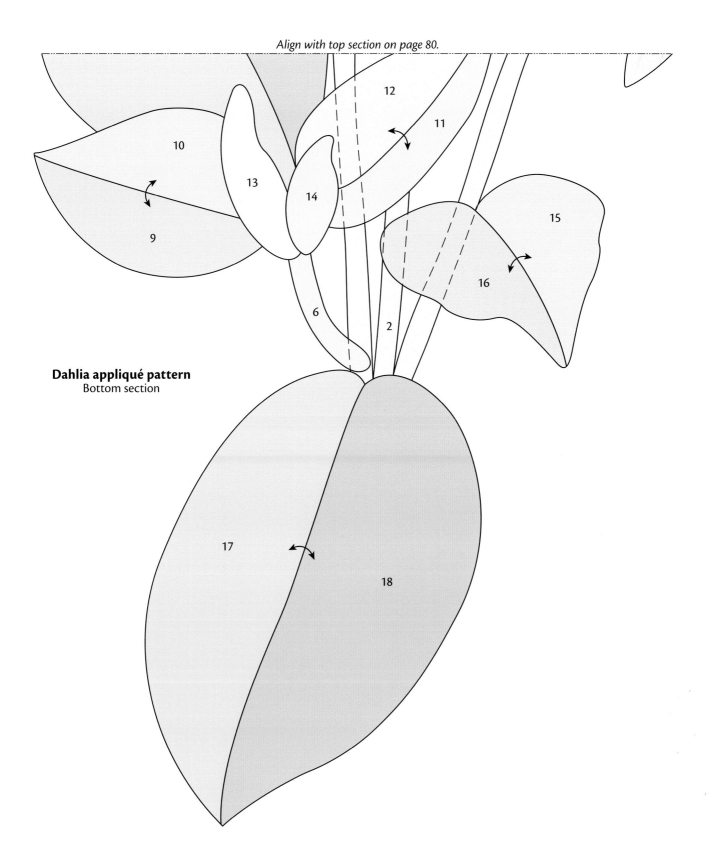

Dahlia appliqué pattern
Bottom section

IVY Zippered Case

If you're a quilter, you know you can never have enough containers to organize all the supplies you need. This zippered case is a good size to hold a number of different items, and it's pretty and easy to make. You can use it to take supplies to quilting classes, and it can also be used as a travel case or cosmetics bag.

Finished size: 5" x 10" x 5"

MATERIALS

All yardages are based on 42"-wide fabric.

½ yard of print fabric for bag background

1 fat eighth of taupe fabric for stems

Scraps of 3 different green fabrics for leaves

16" x 20½" piece of fabric for lining

17" x 22" piece of batting

16" zipper to match bag fabric

Plastic or vinyl for overlay

Freezer paper

CUTTING

All measurements include seam allowances.

From the print fabric, cut:

1 rectangle, 16½" x 21"

1 rectangle, 3" x 8"

APPLIQUÉING THE IVY

Refer to "The Appliqué Process" on page 12.

1. Use the pattern on page 87 to make a complete pattern of the ivy appliqué. Trace the complete pattern onto plastic or vinyl to make the overlay.

2. Use the pattern to make freezer-paper templates for the appliqués. Refer to the color key on page 86 to prepare the appliqués from the fabrics indicated.

3. Refer to the pattern and "Making Bias Strips and Stems" on page 18 to make stem pieces 1–5. Cut the pieces 1" wide for ⅛"-wide finished stems.

4. Fold the print 16½" x 21" rectangle in half lengthwise to find the center. Make a crease. Position the overlay so that the center line is lined up with the center fold on the background rectangle; note the position of the cut edge and seam line. The seam line should be ¼" from the top raw edge.

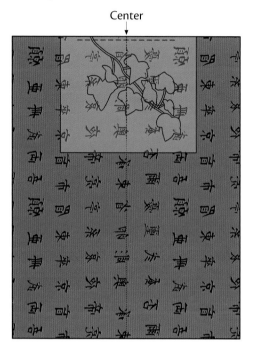

Center

5. Appliqué pieces 1–13 to the background, stitching in numerical order.

6. Remove all freezer-paper templates.

7. Trim the rectangle along the sides and bottom only so that it measures 16" x 20½".

ASSEMBLING THE CASE

1. Layer the appliquéd rectangle with batting; baste the layers together.

2. Quilt as desired. Trim the extra batting.

3. Place the zipper face down along one of the 16" edges of the appliqué front, right sides together. Align the edge of the zipper tape with the raw edges of the fabric. Make sure that the zipper pull is about ¾" from one side and that the zipper stop is not on what will be the ½" seam line on the other side. Using the zipper foot, baste a ¼" seam along the zipper.

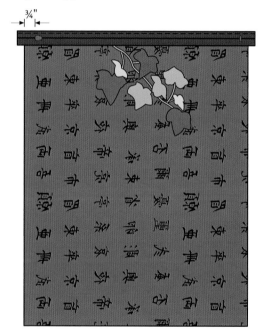

¾"

4. Repeat with the other side of the zipper and the remaining 16" side. You should now have a tube.

5. Place the right side of the lining fabric against the wrong side of the zipper, with the edge of the zipper tape aligned with the raw edges. The zipper is now sandwiched between the lining and the bag front. Stitch a ¼" seam along the zipper.

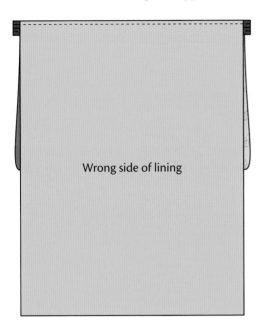

Wrong side of lining

6. Repeat with the other 16" end of the lining and the other side of the zipper. You now have two tubes stitched to the zipper. You can open the zipper if needed when stitching.

7. Turn the outer bag tube inside out so the lining is inside and the zipper is facing out.

8. Open the zipper and press the fabric away from the zipper on both sides. Topstitch ⅛" from the seam.

FINISHING

1. To make the tabs, fold the print 3" x 8" rectangle in half lengthwise, wrong sides together, and press. Then fold each side again toward the center and press.

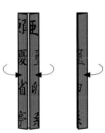

2. Stitch the tab 1/16" from the double-folded edge. Cut into two 4" lengths. Fold each in half to create a tab for each end of the case.

3. Close the zipper. With raw edges aligned, center a tab with both ends of the zipper on the right side of the tube. Baste with a ¼" seam.

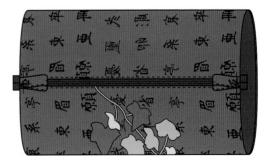

4. Open the zipper and turn the tube inside out. Flatten the tube with the zipper ends centered between the folds. Stitch one side using a ½" seam. Then stitch the other side. Use a zigzag or overlock stitch to secure the raw edges on both sides.

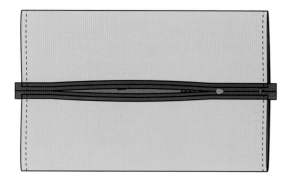

5. Refer to "Making Boxed Corners" on page 26 to form a square corner at each of the four corners of the bag. The distance from the point to the marked line should be 2½" and the corner seam should be 5" long.

COLOR KEY	
Fabric color	**Piece(s)**
Light green	7, 12
Medium-light green	8, 10, 11
Medium green	6, 9, 13
Taupe	1–5

The zippered case can also be made with a bright, decorative fabric.

IVY ZIPPERED CASE

Ivy appliqué pattern

TOP

Cut line

Seam line

Center crease

11

12

13

1

4

10

5

9

8

2

3

7

6

PETUNIA Case

I designed this case so that it can comfortably accommodate a large 60 mm rotary cutter. However, it can hold any size rotary cutter—and even eyeglasses. The fold-over top allows easy access, but prevents a cutter or glasses from sliding out when they're in your bag. I used a lightweight denim for the lining to add to the durability of the case. I used Velcro for the fastener, which is easy to install and won't get snagged in your travel bag.

Finished size: 4½" x 8¼"

MATERIALS

All yardages are based on 42"-wide fabric.

1 fat quarter of blue print for cover

1 fat quarter of coordinating blue print for lining

Scraps of 3 different salmon-pink fabrics for flower

Scraps of 4 different green fabrics for leaves and stems

Scrap of burgundy fabric for flower center

Scrap of very pale-green fabric for flower center

⅛ yard of fabric for binding

⅜ yard or craft pack of heavyweight interfacing such as Timtex

1" piece of ¾"-wide Velcro for fastener

Plastic or vinyl for overlay

Freezer paper

CUTTING

All measurements include seam allowances.

From the blue print for cover, cut:

1 rectangle, 5" x 8¾"

1 rectangle, 5" x 12¾"

From the interfacing, cut:

1 rectangle, 5" x 8¾"

1 rectangle, 5" x 12¾"

From the coordinating blue print, cut:

1 rectangle, 5" x 8¾"

1 rectangle, 5" x 12¾"

From the binding fabric, cut:

1 strip, 2¼" x 42"

APPLIQUÉING THE COVER

Refer to "The Appliqué Process" on page 12.

1. Use the pattern on pages 92 and 93 to make a complete pattern of the petunia appliqué. Trace the complete pattern onto plastic or vinyl to make the overlay.

2. Use the pattern to make freezer-paper templates for the appliqués. Refer to the color key on page 91 to prepare the appliqués from the fabrics indicated.

3. Refer to the pattern and "Making Bias Strips and Stems" on page 18 to make stem pieces 3 and 9. Cut the pieces 1¼" wide for ¼"-wide finished stems.

4. Appliqué the following pieces together to make units: 4 and 5, and 7 and 8.

5. Appliqué pieces 1–8 to the 5" x 8¾" blue print rectangle for the cover, stitching in numerical order.

6. Position the overlay for the petunia on the 5" x 12¾" rectangle so that the bottom line of the pattern is on the bottom short edge of the rectangle. Appliqué pieces 9–16, stitching in numerical order.

CONSTRUCTING THE CASE

1. Position the rough half of the Velcro strip onto the right side of the larger coordinating lining piece so that it's about ½" from the top edge and centered side to side. Stitch ⅛" from the edge all the way around the Velcro.

2. Layer each of the two appliquéd pieces, wrong sides together, with the corresponding lining piece. Insert the corresponding piece of interfacing between the layers and baste the layers together.

3. Quilt as desired. Trim any extra interfacing and lining fabric from the two rectangles.

4. Center the remaining half of the Velcro piece on the right side of the appliquéd leaf rectangle, with the top edge of the Velcro piece approximately 2¼" from the top of the rectangle and centered from side to side. Place the leaf rectangle on the lining side of the other quilted rectangle and fold the petunia rectangle over to check that the Velcro pieces meet. Reposition as needed, remove the leaf rectangle, and stitch ⅛" from the edge all the way around the Velcro.

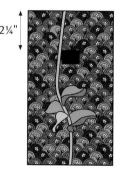

PETUNIA CASE

FINISHING

1. Refer to "Binding" on page 23 to add binding to the top edge only of the smaller leaf rectangle.

2. Position the smaller leaf rectangle so that the bottom is aligned with the bottom of the large petunia rectangle, lining sides together. Baste together along the sides and bottom.

3. Add binding to the outer edges of the case.

COLOR KEY	
Fabric color	**Piece(s)**
Light salmon pink	13, 16
Medium-light salmon pink	11, 12
Medium salmon pink	10
Burgundy	14
Light green	6
Medium-light green	1, 2, 7
Medium green	4, 5, 8
Pale green	3, 9
Very pale green	15

A border print or a striped fabric works well for the rotary-cutter case.

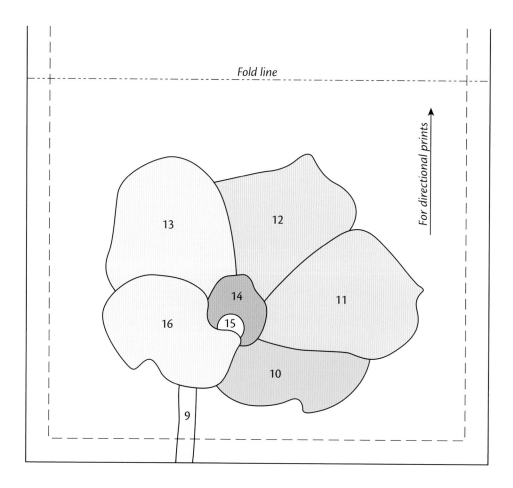

Fold line

For directional prints

Petunia appliqué pattern
Top section

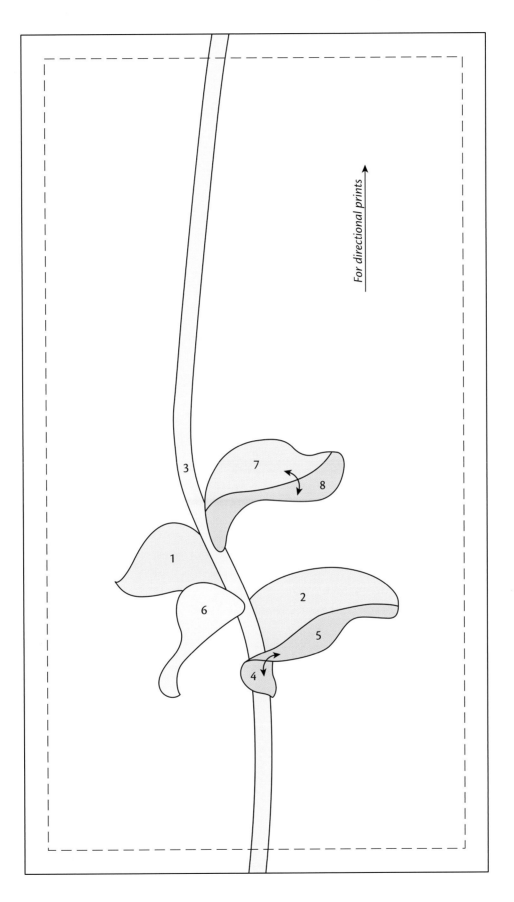

For directional prints

Petunia appliqué pattern
Bottom section

PETUNIA CASE

— Swan and Nessie LAYOUT—

You can use this diagram to create your own version of "Swan and Nessie," shown on page 7. Use the full-sized patterns throughout the book and add your own mountains, trees, and other flora as desired. For the inner border, cut strips 1¼" wide to finish at ¾". Cut outer-border strips 3½" wide to finish at 3".

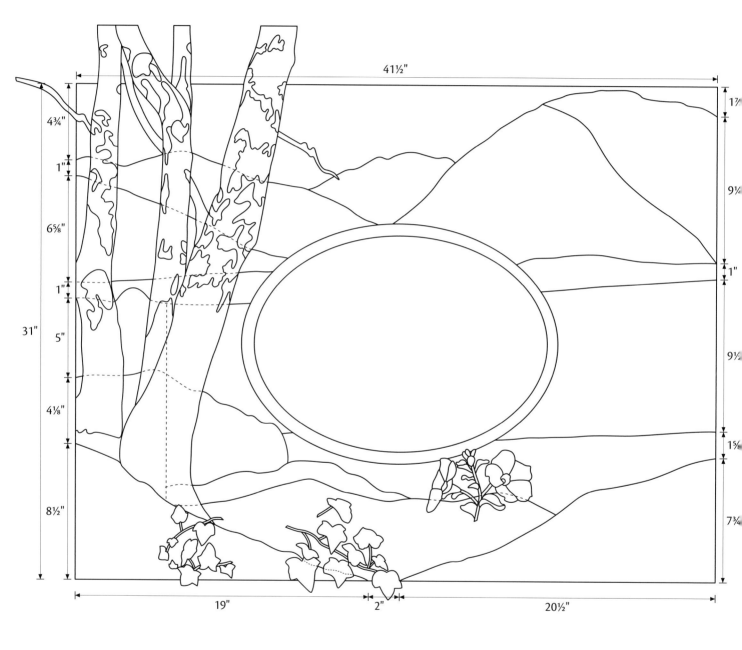

Meet the AUTHOR

Photo by Kerry Grant

Susan Taylor Propst learned to quilt in 1987 when she was expecting her first child. She began her career as a quilting teacher in 1994 while living in rural Colorado. Initially she started teaching because she didn't have anyone nearby to share quilting with, but soon she was able to form a small quilting group. In 1999, she and her family moved to northern England, and she quickly resumed her teaching pursuits. While in England, she completed City & Guilds in Patchwork and Quilting, and in 2006 Susan received a Higher National Certificate in Textiles. (City & Guilds is an organization that awards vocational qualifications. Students learn techniques, design, and fabric coloration.) In late 2009, Susan and her family relocated back to the United States. She enjoys teaching all levels of quilters and has been popular with her students, both British and American. Although she likes all aspects of quilting, she's particularly fond of appliqué and enjoys designing patterns. This is Susan's third book, and her third partnership with That Patchwork Place. Her first book is *Beautiful Blooms: Quilts and Cushions to Appliqué* and her second book is *Another Season of Beautiful Blooms: Appliquéd Quilts and Cushions*. Susan also designs numerous patterns for her students to use in classes. She currently lives in Colorado Springs, Colorado, with her husband and the youngest of their three children.

There's More Online!

To see more of Susan's designs or to learn about her workshops, visit www.susantaylorpropst.com.

See other quilting books, including Susan's previous titles, at www.martingale-pub.com.

YOU MIGHT ALSO ENJOY THESE OTHER FINE TITLES FROM
Martingale & Company

Our books are available at bookstores and your favorite craft, fabric, and yarn retailers.
Visit us at www.martingale-pub.com or contact us at:

1-800-426-3126
International: 1-425-483-3313
Fax: 1-425-486-7596
Email: info@martingale-pub.com

Martingale®
& C O M P A N Y

America's Best-Loved Craft & Hobby Books®
America's Best-Loved Knitting Books®

America's Best-Loved Quilt Books®